UNDERSTANDING HALAL FOODS
Fallacies and Facts

Ahmad H. Sakr, Ph.D.

Copyright 1996
All Rights Reserved

UNDERSTANDING HALAL FOODS
FALLACIES AND FACTS

Library of Congress Catalog Card Number
96-61717

ISBN
0-911119-76-0

By

Ahmad H. Sakr Ph.D.

Published By:

Foundation For Islamic Knowledge
P.O. Box 665
Lombard, IL. 60148
Phone (630) 495-4817
Fax (630) 627-8894
Tax I.D. # 36-352-8916

Note: Your generous contribution to the above foundations will enable us to publish more valuable literature and to render more services to all. Your donations are tax deductible.

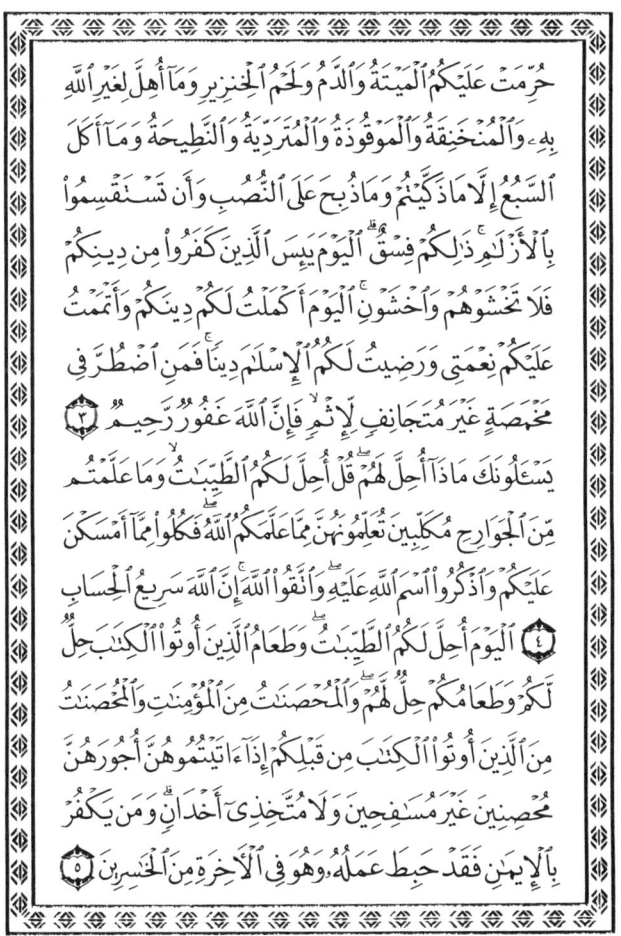

Translation of the Qur'an: Chapter 5, Verses 3, 4, and 5.

Forbidden to you (for food) are: dead meat, blood, the flesh of swine, and that on which has been invoked the name of other than Allah (swt); that which has been killed by strangling, or by a violent blow, or by a headlong fall, or by being gored to death; that which has been (partly) eaten by a wild animal; unless you are able to slaughter it (in due form); that which is sacrificed on stone (altars); (forbidden) also is the division (of meat) by raffling with arrows; that is impiety. This day have those who reject faith given up all hope of your religion: Yet fear them not but fear Me. This day have I perfected your religion for you, completed My favour upon you, and have chosen for you Islam as your religion. But if any is forced by hunger, with no inclination to transgression, Allah (swt) is indeed oft forgiving, most merciful.

They ask them what is lawful to them (as food). Say: lawful unto you are (all) things good and pure: and what you have taught the beasts and birds of prey, training them to hunt in the manner directed to you by Allah (swt): Eat what they catch for you, but pronounce the name of Allah (swt) over it: and fear Allah (swt); for Allah (swt) is swift in taking account.

This day are (all) things Good and pure made lawful unto you. The food of the people of the book is lawful unto you and yours is lawful unto them. (Lawful unto you in marriage are (not only) chaste women who are believers, but chaste women among the people of the book, revealed before your time,- when you give them their due dowers, and desire chastity, not lewdness. Taking them as lovers. In any one rejects faith, fruitless is his work, and in the Hereafter he will be in the ranks of those who have lost (all spiritual good).

ACKNOWLEDGMENTS

The Author wishes to thank all those friends who helped in making this book available to the readers.

Special thanks to Dr. and Mrs. Mohammad Shafi and their family, as well as to the Al-Qur'an Foundation of Milwaukee, Wisconsin, for their tremendous help in publishing this particular book and the upcoming few books Insha'allah. The author is very thankful to them. May Allah bless and reward them.

The author wishes to thank Dr. Yusuf Kamaluddin (Yao-Keng) Chang and his wife, Audrey, for their tremendous help and moral support during the last few years.

Thanks and appreciation go to FAITH (Foundation of American Islamic Teachings & Heritage and their Board members, especially the Vakil brothers (Abu Bakr, Usman, Farooq, Ishaq, Iqbal, and their support to the author and the Foundation to publish his previous books. To them they made it as a Sadaqah Jariyah (perpetual charity) on behalf of their late parents Umar and Amina Vakil. May Allah bless their souls and grant them paradise. May Allah reward the Vakil families for their support. The foundation encourages friends of the Foundation to follow suit.

Moreover, the author wishes to thank all the respected brothers and sisters who have helped previously and are still helping. Among the many are Mr. & Mrs. Javed Habib, Mr. & Mrs. Abdul Wahab, Mr. & Mrs. Saghir Aslam, Dr. & Mrs. Nadim Daouk, Dr. & Mrs. Arshud Mahmood, Mr. Refat M. Abo Elela, Dr. & Mrs. Zeyd A. Merenkov, Mr. & Mrs. Asad Khan, Mr. Feroz Battla and his wife Dr. Hamida Battla, Mr. & Mrs. Atiq jilani and many more.

Last but not least, the author wishes to thank his loving wife Zuhar Barhumi Sakr and the loving children Sara, Hussein, Jihad and Basil.

May Allah bless all those who contributed their time, effort, energy, wealth, wisdom, goodwill, artwork, editing, typing, proofreading, printing, and in the their Du'a'. Special thanks and appreciation goes to Sister Nadia Hassan for her sincere efforts and hardwork in typing, proofreading and designing. Moreso, for her advice and suggestions in improving certain items. May Allah (swt) bless her and her mother, Shadia Hassan, for her help and contributions for the love of Allah. Finally our prayers of Maghfirah for the husband of sister Shadia. His name is Mr. Samir Hassan. May Allah (swt) bless his soul and make his final stay in Paradise. Ameen!

Special Prayer

The author prays to Allah (swt)[1] to bless Prophet Muhammad (pbuh)[2] and the family of Prophet Muhammad. The author also prays to Allah (swt) to bless the Khulafaa' Rashidoon and the Sahaba of the Prophet as well as the followers (Tabi'oon) and the followers of the followers till the Day of Judgment.

The author prays to Allah (swt) to reward his parents: his late father Al-Hajj Hussain Mustafa Sakr and his late mother Al-Hajjah Sara Ramadan Sakr for their sacrifices to their children in general and to this author in specific. The author prays to Allah (swt) to reward the late brother of the author, Mr. Muhammad H. Sakr, for helping the author to get his academic education, and his late brother Mahmood H. Sakr, for taking care of the author's responsibility overseas.

Special prayers go to the Sheikh of the author who taught him Islam, and trained him from childhood to practice its teachings: Sheikh Muhammad 'Umar Daouq. May Allah be pleased with him. Special Du'a' goes to Al-Shaheed Sheikh Hassan Khalid, the late Grand Mufti of Lebanon, who had also great impact on the author's knowledge of Islam. May Allah bless his soul and make him stay in Paradise.

---

[1] swt: Subhanahu Wa Ta'ala (Glory Be To Allah, and He is the High)

[2] pbuh: Peace Be Upon Him (The Prophet)

Special prayers and Du'a' go to the many teachers, scholars and 'Ulama' who were directly tutoring at the time of his youth. Through the efforts of Sheikh Muhammad Umar Daouq, the following is a partial list of the teachers who taught this author: Dr. Mustafa Siba'ee; Sheikh Muhammad M. Al-Sawwaf; Dr. Muhammad Al-Zo'bee; Sh. Muhammad Itani; Sh. Muhammad A.K. Khattabi; Sh. Malik Bennabi; Sh. Faheem Abu'Ubeyh; Sh. Muhammad Al-Shaal; Dr. Saeed Ramadan; Atty. Abdel Hakeem Abideen; Dr. Tawfic Houri; Sh. 'Umar Houri; Sh. Abu Salih Itani; Sh. Hashim Daftardar Al-Madani and Sheikh Abdul Badee' Sakr. May Allah bless and reward them all.

A final prayer is to the Reader who took the time to read this book. May Allah (swt) bless all Insha'Allah.

Allahumma   Ameen.

Understanding Halal Foods

TABLE OF CONTENTS

I.	Introduction		1
II.	Concerns		6
	A.	General	6
	B.	Specific Concerns	7
	C.	More Concerns	8
	D.	Concerns of the Author	20
	E.	IFANCA's Concerns	21
III.	Halal and Haram Defined		23
IV.	General Concepts		31
V.	Fallacies and Facts		33
	A.	Muslim Foods	33
	B.	Zabiha and Halal	35
	C.	Slaughtering Animals	37
	D.	Kosher Foods	38
	E.	Supermarket Meats	39
	F.	Vegetarian Foods	40
	G.	Sea Foods	41
	H.	Choosing wrong food Products	42

VI.	Strategy For Better Health		47
	A.	General	47
	B.	Beware	48
	C.	Alternatives	49
VII.	Improving Food Values		51
VIII.	Recommendations		53
	A.	Consumers	53
	B.	Food Industries	54
	C.	Muslim Countries	55
IX.	Final Remarks		57
	Addendum		60
		A. Kosher Gelatin	60
		B. Ingredients vs. Products	62
		C. From Haram to Halal	65
		D. List of Halal-Haram Ingredients	70
		E. Halal Milk	75
		F. Mad Cow	80
		G. Is Halal Supervision Necessary	86
		H. Pork slaughtered according to Islamic Shariah	88
		I. Vitamins	92
		J. USDA & Muslim Foods	100
		K. Diet of Muslims Inmates	111
	References		115
	Foundation		121
	List of Published Books		126
	Books To Be Published		129

I
INTRODUCTION

Muslims throughout history and throughout the different parts of the world are concerned about the Halal and the Haram. Among other things they are concerned about is eating the Halal foods and drinking Halal liquids. They are also to earn through Halal methods, as well as to spend their money, time, effort, energy, and knowledge through Halal approaches. The Qur'an is explicit about eating Halal. In Surah Al-Baqarah Allah (swt) says the following:

يَـٰٓأَيُّهَا ٱلنَّاسُ كُلُواْ مِمَّا فِى ٱلْأَرْضِ حَلَـٰلًا طَيِّبًا وَلَا تَتَّبِعُواْ خُطُوَٰتِ ٱلشَّيْطَـٰنِ إِنَّهُۥ لَكُمْ عَدُوٌّ مُّبِينٌ ۝

O you people! Eat of what is on earth, lawful and good; and do not follow the footsteps of Satan for he is to you an avowed enemy. [2:168]

The Legislator of Halal and Haram in Islam is only Allah (swt). Prophet Muhammad (pbuh) was the only one who had the right to explain the Qur'an, to interpret it, and to deliver it. He lived it and delivered it to all.

Through science and technology, foods have been processed by many techniques. After that they are shipped to different parts of the world. New food products are also developed through the use of new techniques, approaches, and methods. The non-Muslims countries have become the major producing of industrial and technological materials, while the Muslims in the Muslim world stayed as consumers. Majority of the non-Muslims do not have the concept of Halal/Haram, while to the Muslims, this concept is very important.

For the last century, the Muslim have been receiving so many food products that contain alcohol, pork, and ingredients that are Haram. Sometimes the processing techniques, as well as the containers, the preservatives and the additives may contain Haram materials. Most of the Muslims in the Muslim world did not know what is going on. They did not expect that Haram ingredients were added to the food products. At the beginning, Food Labeling was not even an issue to the Muslim world. The same is to be said about processing techniques, the packaging, and many other terminologies. Such issues could be synthetic vs. natural; inorganic vs. organic; coloring dyes vs. flavoring aromas; and so on and so forth.

Muslims of North America have increased in number since World War I and especially after World War II. As of year 1996, their number exceeds 6 to 8 millions and they are scattered all over the continent in large and small cities. The majority of these Muslims are immigrants and their descendants. There are 35% to 40% Americans and Canadians who accepted Islam.

Those who migrated are from most of the Muslim countries such as Arab lands, Pakistan, India, Bangladesh, Burma, Africa, China, Cambodia, Vietnam, Philippines, Indonesia, Malaysia, Turkey, Russia, Albania, Bosnia, Iran, etc. These Muslims brought with them their schools of thought (Hanafi, Shafii, Hanbali, Maliki, and Jafari [Shiites]) along with their customs, habits, and traditions. They are highly educated in science and technology, but not in matters of Shari'ah. They have, however, the love for their religion.

Those who accepted Islam are mainly the African-Americans, the Hispanics, and the Caucasians. These new Muslims have had different customs, habits, and food requirements. They had to readapt their food habits and requirements to the Islamic Shari'ah. It was not easy for them because it took time to find out the true information as well as the availability of Halal food stores. However, they were able to add different varieties of menus to their own food. Lately they transcended all types of difficulties and were able to practice the teachings of Islam concerning Halal food.

As far as the concept of Halal food is concerned, Muslims are not yet in agreement with one another. Their understanding of each other's school of thought is also not clear. Some disagree with the interpretation of the Islamic teachings with others who are of the same school. Hence, it is up to the individuals to act independently.

As far as the presence of 'Ulama' in Shari'ah is concerned, some of them added to the confusion among the Muslim masses. Most of these 'Ulama' are not aware about the legality of the processes of slaughtering in North America. They built their understanding from someone who informed them his own version of slaughtering. Hence, their Fatwa and opinions are built upon the wrong information they got through some friends.

Finally, the Muslims of North America became divided. Some consider the meat in the market is totally Haram, while others consider it totally Halal. Those in between consider it Mashbooh or Makrooh. Some Muslims decided that kosher meat is Halal while the meat of Christians is not Halal. The result is a chaos and a confusion.

In such a state of confusion, a large number of Muslim grocery stores started selling Halal meat. Each Muslim meat store claims that the meat he sells is totally Zabiha and Halal. Whether his claim is right or questionable, the validity of his claim does need to be verified.

Some Muslim intellectuals and scholars in the fields of science and technology were committed to their Faith. They were able to bring these issues and problems to the attention of the Muslims in the Muslim world. They were able to see a sign of awakening toward Halal/Haram issues in matters of foods, liquids, smoking, medicine, pharmaceutical drugs, vitamins, minerals, enzymes, co-enzymes, processing techniques, lining, packaging, slaughtering, shipment, storage, and so on and so forth. Hence, Muslims in the Muslim world as well as those living in the non-Muslim societies started demanding from the industries to have Halal products. The industries started answering some of the demands of the Muslim consumers. The more Muslims demand as consumers, the more the industries will be willing to produce Halal food products.

It is through education and communications that people in different parts of the world will be able to understand each other. Through honesty and sincerity, both the industries and the consumers will benefit from one another. A better way of life will be established where all are sharing the responsibilities and caring for one another.

In this book, the author is to expand on the concept of **Fallacies and Facts** in matters of foods and liquids. He will bring some of the wrong ideas (Myths) to the attention of Muslims, and explain how far those ideas are true or not. Then he will try to bring about the realities of these items. In so doing, a better picture will be in front of the consumers. Then the consumers will be intelligent enough to select and reject independently according to their needs and within the framework of their faith.

We pray to Allah to accept our efforts and to forgive our shortcomings.

There is no deity but Allah, and Muhammad is the Messenger of Allah.

II
CONCERNS

A.   General.   Many groups of people in America are concerned about the food they eat.

1.   Jews are concerned if the food is kosher or not.

2.   Hindus and Buddhists are concerned about their food to be vegetarian.

3.   Seventh Day Adventists are concerned about having no meat in the foods, too.

4.   Certain groups are concerned about chemical preservatives on foods as well as the type of fertilizers used for plants and feeds for animals.

5.   Muslims are concerned about the foods being Halal. If animals are to be used, they have to be slaughtered according to Islamic Shari'ah. Other food items should be devoid of pork, ham, lard, bacon, and other bi-products of the pig. The food has to be free of any alcohol or alcoholic bi-products in order to be Halal.

There are foods that may contain certain types of ingredients extracted from Haram sources such as enzymes, lecithin, mono- and di-glycerides, glycogen, lard, shortenings, whey, vitamins, minerals, amino aides, fatty acids, alcohol of different natures, etc. There are compound derivatives of Haram products. There are also medicinal products that contain alcohol or even the gelatinous capsules are made of pork fat. More recent concerns are the tin cans and steel drums which are laminated from inside with glossy materials that contain pork fat, too.

With the complexity of the matter, some individuals have to take the initiative to do something about it. They have to inform the public as well as the Muslims about the problems. They have to show them the alternatives as well.

B. **Specific Concerns.** Muslims are concerned of every food and liquid sold in the market. Their concerns are related to the following:

1. **Food items:** Whether they have pork, hams, bacon, lard, shortenings (vegetable, animals, etc.), mono- and di-glycerides, gelatin, enzymes (rennin, rennet, microbial, plants), lecithin, and other types of ingredients, additives or preservatives.

2. **Meat:** Whether the animals are slaughtered according to Islamic Shari'ah, or not. Whether they are fed Halal foods, and whether hormones are injected into them or not.

3. **Liquids:** Those liquids may contain alcohol, caffeine, and tannin; and

4. **Packaging:** If the containers are metal, then whether the lining is from synthetic minerals, vegetables oils, or animal products.

C.   **More Concerns.**

1.   **Labeling:**   The Food and Drug Administration (FDA) of U.S.A. maintains strict control over labeling of food and drugs. However, labeling on a food product may sometimes be misleading. At the same time, nothing is mentioned about the source of some of the ingredients. The source of natural instead of synthetic flavors or colors could be from insects, animals (including pork), or plants. The source of organic instead of inorganic could also be from animals, insects or plants. Therefore, it is a concern for all of the Muslims in different parts of the world. It is their responsibility to demand Halal sources.

2.   **Food Ingredients:**   In 1973 a new legislation was introduced by the FDA (Food and Drug Administration) requiring a food processor to reveal a full declaration of the nutritional information regarding the products processed. They legislated that the new U.S. Recommended Dietary Allowance (U.S. RDA) replaces the Minimum Daily Requirements (MDR) as standard for labeling purposes.

The concern of consumers is that there are many ingredients being used in the food industry. It is not easy for everyone to know all of them. Someone who is knowledgeable in the subject and in Islamic Shari'ah has to volunteer his services to write about this subject. The author of this book is one of the very few who wrote on this subject. The consumers are advised to read his writings on the subject.

Some of the ingredients might be food ingredients, food supplements, additives, preservatives or cosmetics, coloring materials or flavors and aroma. Some might be toxic, others might be added from a Haram source into the food products.

3. **Side Effects of Additives:** Food additives are added in small quantities, but some people cannot tolerate them. They may be sensitive to them and, hence, they may be poisoned with their presence in foods.

Sometimes the dangers from these additives are possibly tangible. The presence of nitrites -- nitrites in meats may produce cancer.

4. **Hormones:** The injection of Diethyl Stilbestrol (DES) female hormones in beef and chicken may increase homosexuality in male children. During the Reagan Administration, the European meat market refused to buy American beef and chickens because of the presence of growth hormone in them. The American farmers were using DES hormone into these animals, and as such, the USDA has to demand from the American farmers not to use this growth hormone (female sex hormone). Although it became a law, a good number of farmers are still using DES. There is no way that a Doctor of Veterinary Medicine (DVM) will discover it during the slaughtering time.

5. **Other chemicals:** The intake of saccharine may produce

cancer. The use of cyclamates in rats in high doses were correlated with cancer production. Some dyes in foods were found to cause cancer in lab animals. The use of caffeine in diets may produce deformities in the fetus of expecting mothers.

The subject of food additives is very important to everyone -- consumers, FDA and the food industry. It is, therefore, very pertinent to request every consumer to read the ingredients on the labels. It is important also to read literature about every ingredient including the additives. It is further requested that the consumer makes it a habit to read the label on every item purchased.

6. **Dairy Products:** Among the dairy products are milk, yogurt (Laban), strained yogurt (Labnah), cheeses, whey, milk butter, cottage cheese, etc. Milk and milk products are being used in many pastries, confectioneries, breads, cookies, cakes, powdered milk, skim milk, concentrated milk, evaporated milk, etc.

Consumers are worried as to the methods used in preparing all these food products. Their concerns are valid when it comes to whey, cheeses, milk, butter, margarine, etc. Their concerns are based on Halal / Haram, Zabiha, and also on health reasons. One has to find the source of these products and their degree of Halal, Haram, Mashbooh, or Makrooh.

7. **Cheese:** Many people in different parts of the world are concerned about the method of cheese preparation. The process of curdling of the casein protein does necessitate the use of enzymes,

acid, microbes, or vegetable juices. Most companies have been using animal enzymes, such as pepsin, rennin or rennet. These enzymes are obtained from the stomach of pig (porcine, rennin, rennet) or calf. All those Muslims who are looking for Halal ingredients from Zabiha / Halal animals should refuse to eat any cheese made through such a process.

The use of microbial enzymes is now widely used in the preparation of cheeses. Such use of enzymes should be considered Halal.

Lemon juice, as an acid to curdle and coagulate the milk, is being used on a small scale for the vegetarians, as well as for those who are interested in natural and organic materials. The use of raw fig juice (white sap) extract has also been used for the vegetarians and consumers who are interested in the natural / organic products.

Consumers are requested to verify from the cheese companies and the pizza stores as to the source of their products.

8.   **Milk:** There is a variety of milk in the market. The most important and the most predominant is cow's milk. This is the main milk that people do drink, and from which many dairy products are produced.

Infants are recommended to be nursed by their mother's milk. In Surah Al-Baqarah (The Cow), Allah (swt) says the following:

﷽ وَٱلْوَٰلِدَٰتُ يُرْضِعْنَ أَوْلَٰدَهُنَّ حَوْلَيْنِ كَامِلَيْنِ ۖ لِمَنْ أَرَادَ أَن يُتِمَّ ٱلرَّضَاعَةَ ۚ وَعَلَى ٱلْمَوْلُودِ لَهُۥ رِزْقُهُنَّ وَكِسْوَتُهُنَّ بِٱلْمَعْرُوفِ ۚ لَا تُكَلَّفُ نَفْسٌ إِلَّا وُسْعَهَا ۚ لَا تُضَآرَّ وَٰلِدَةٌۢ بِوَلَدِهَا وَلَا مَوْلُودٌ لَّهُۥ بِوَلَدِهِۦ ۚ وَعَلَى ٱلْوَارِثِ مِثْلُ ذَٰلِكَ ۗ فَإِنْ أَرَادَا فِصَالًا عَن تَرَاضٍ مِّنْهُمَا وَتَشَاوُرٍ فَلَا جُنَاحَ عَلَيْهِمَا ۗ وَإِنْ أَرَدتُّمْ أَن تَسْتَرْضِعُوٓا۟ أَوْلَٰدَكُمْ فَلَا جُنَاحَ عَلَيْكُمْ إِذَا سَلَّمْتُم مَّآ ءَاتَيْتُم بِٱلْمَعْرُوفِ ۗ وَٱتَّقُوا۟ ٱللَّهَ وَٱعْلَمُوٓا۟ أَنَّ ٱللَّهَ بِمَا تَعْمَلُونَ بَصِيرٌ ﴿٢٣٣﴾

The mothers shall give suck to their offspring for two whole years, for him who desires to complete the term. But he shall bear the cost of their food and clothing on equitable terms. No soul shall have a burden laid on it greater than it can bear. No mother shall be treated unfairly on account of her child. Nor father on account of his child, an heir shall be chargeable in the same way. If they both decide on weaning, by mutual consent, and after due consultation. There is no blame on them if ye decide on a foster-mother for your offspring there is no blame on you, provided you pay (the *foster mother) what you offered, on equitable terms. But fear Allah (swt) and know that Allah (swt) sees well what you do.* [2:233]

The latter is far better for the health and emotional of the baby. At the same time, mother's milk has better nutritional values than cow's milk. If a mother cannot nurse her baby another mother should nurse him. In the Qur'an, Allah (swt) says the following in Surah Al-Talaq (Divorce):

$$\text{أَسْكِنُوهُنَّ مِنْ حَيْثُ سَكَنتُم مِّن وُجْدِكُمْ وَلَا تُضَآرُّوهُنَّ لِتُضَيِّقُوا۟ عَلَيْهِنَّ ۚ وَإِن كُنَّ أُو۟لَٰتِ حَمْلٍ فَأَنفِقُوا۟ عَلَيْهِنَّ حَتَّىٰ يَضَعْنَ حَمْلَهُنَّ ۚ فَإِنْ أَرْضَعْنَ لَكُمْ فَـَٔاتُوهُنَّ أُجُورَهُنَّ ۖ وَأْتَمِرُوا۟ بَيْنَكُم بِمَعْرُوفٍ ۖ وَإِن تَعَاسَرْتُمْ فَسَتُرْضِعُ لَهُۥٓ أُخْرَىٰ ۝٦}$$

Let the women live (in 'iddat) in the same style as you live, according to your means: Annoy them not, so as to restrict them. And if they are pregnant, then spend (your substance) on them until they deliver their burden: and if they suckle your (offspring), give them their recompense: and take mutual counsel together, according to what is just and reasonable. And if you find yourselves in difficulties, let another women suckle (the child) on the (father's) behalf. [65:6]

Cow's milk usually has 4% fat. Since people are worried about cholesterol and fat in their diet, industries tried to reduce the concentration of fat to 2%, 1%, or skim milk.

Recently the FDA of USA has granted the permission for the American farmers to inject estrogen (EST) into the cows. Such permission was granted in February 1994. The hormone EST does increase the productivity of milk from the cows as well as the size of the milk bladder. The government agency required that milk bottles from such approach should have the symbol of EST; later on FDA did not require such a demand.

The concern of all consumers (Muslims & non-Muslims) from all over the world is about the presence of female hormone (EST) in the milk. Since people are drinking milk on a daily basis, they are ingesting more female hormones in their bodies. This concern is valid for both males and females. Their concern is what is going to happen to them physiologically, biologically, genetically, emotionally, and physically. Would such a hormone increase the breast of a women? Would such a hormone start forming breasts for young men, too? If yes, what should men do? It would be too late to wait and see. One has to do something about it now before it happens.

9.   **Whey:**   "Milk Serum" is the liquid that remains after the

curd and the cream are removed from the coagulation of the casein of milk. Coagulation takes place either for cheese or yogurt preparation. Whey contains most of the sugar lactose of the original milk but has little protein and very little fat.

Curdling of milk for cheese preparation takes place with the use of the enzyme rennin (rennet). Whey produced is, therefore, to be suspected, because the source of rennin could be animal. The animal used could be hogs. The consumer is advised to ask the food industry about the source of rennin whenever whey is included as part of the ingredients.

10. Gelatin: A product obtained (by boiling in water) from the partial hydrolysis of collagen derived from cartilages, bones, tendons and skin of animals. Gelatin swells up when put in cold water, but dissolves only in hot water. Although a protein of animal origin, it is of poor biological value and is considered an incomplete protein. It lacks tryptophan (essential amino acid) and is low in cystine and tyrosine. It is used as a protein food adjunct in malnutrition areas.

Vegetable gelatin is similar to animal gelatin in its function and is obtained from gluten of wheat or other cereals. Gelatin is used in the food industry extensively and among the most famous product is Jell-O. However, Jell-O can be made of agar-agar derived from seaweed (various red algae). Agar-agar is also used as a solidifying agent in culture media. Gelatin is used in confectionery, jellies and ice creams. This is also as a clarifying agent in the food industry.

Kosher gelatin is NOT Halal for Muslims as it may contain pork collagen.[3] To some liberal Jews, it is kosher; while to the conservative Jews, it is NOT kosher.

Every concerned consumer should be worried about the use and the consumption of any food or diet that contains gelatin. One has to find out whether the source of gelatin is plant, animal or seaweed. If the source is animal, one has to ask whether pork bi-products have been used. Those Muslims who look for `Zabiha' meat should also insist that gelatin must be derived from `Zabiha' animals. One should not be concerned only for `Zabiha' meat but also for the by-products of meat.

11.   Rennin (Rennet):   These two terms mean the same thing. Rennin is used more in scientific writings while rennet is used in the food industry. Rennin is also called chymosin or chymase. It is a protein enzyme present as such or as zymogen (precursor) in the cells of gastric tubules of small animals' stomachs. In calf it is found in the glandular layer of the stomach.

Rennet as an enzyme, is used in the food industry for the preparation of cheeses by curdling the milk. It is sold for the making of junket or rennet custards. Recently rennet is produced from plants or microbes. The only way to know whether

---

[3] See statement at the end of this book.

the source of rennet is animal, plant or microbe is to ask the food industry about it or else it is written on the label. For instance, Hansen's Laboratory, Inc. in Milwaukee, Wisconsin produces plant and animal cheese rennet tablets. In order to recognize that the rennet is from plant origin, the company has written on the label "Hannilase Rennet;" otherwise, it is made of animal, namely, calf. They do not use pork rennet.

12. **Pepsin:** A digestive enzyme (protease) of the gastric juices, formed from pepsinogen. It hydrolyses peptide bonds of the proteins, thus reducing them to smaller molecules (peptones). Pepsin is commercially prepared from swine (hog, pig) stomachs, which on the average give about one gram of pepsin from one stomach. Calf pepsin is also prepared on a small scale.

There is a great concern among Muslim and non-Muslim consumers regarding pepsin and its utilization in foods and beverages. Some people quit eating and drinking these food and beverages that do or may contain pepsin. The only way to recognize if pepsin is from pig or calf is to read the label on the food products. If the information on the label does not mention the source, then one has to ask the food industry in order to verify the source of pepsin before jumping to a wrong conclusion.

13. **Organic vs. synthetic:** There are many consumers who are confused when told that organic products such as vitamins are better than synthetic. In reality all organic vitamins in the market are

all synthetic ones. The FDA allows the industry to name the vitamins to be organic if they add to the synthetic ones any of the following:
- a. yeast
- b. liver extract
- c. rose hips; or
- d. any of the natural organic bases.

The industry cannot afford to extract natural organic vitamins from the plants of the world so as to put them on shelves. They synthesize vitamins easily and add natural organic bases to them. Nothing is better than the other. Chemically both are the same. Biologically and metabolically, they are also the same. The only difference would be the natural additives found in the organic over the synthetic ones, which are not significantly better.

14.   Natural vs. Chemical: There are many health food stores in America. They claim that the foods they sell are of better quality. One of the reasons, as they say, is because the foods are natural. The concerns of the Muslims: Is it true that natural foods are of better quality? The reality is as follows:

Foods grown on farms are considered natural. If plants are given manure, they are considered to be grown naturally; but if they were given chemical fertilizers, they are not considered to be natural because they are not fed with organic fertilizers.

Plants grown on organic fertilizers tend to give fruits which are concentrated with good flavor and aroma, but the fruits will be smaller in size. The plants grown with chemical fertilizers tend to give large fruits that have less aroma and flavor.

The quality of fruit from the first type of fertilizers may be considered high in ratio and proportion because the fruits are smaller in size and, hence, have better taste and flavor.

We have to remember that the fruits, if not sprayed with pesticides, may be damaged, and indeed, a substantial quantity is being lost due to infestation with pests.

Natural dried fruits are dried by the sun in the open air. This method of natural drying of fruits and vegetables tends to bring the quality down due to the method of heating or drying. In the daytime, heat from the sun tends to dry the fruits while at night, the temperature is low. Anytime, a method of drying through the use of heating and cooling (as is the method of sun drying) will destroy the vitamins very quickly. This means that the quality of the natural dried fruits is low.

Dried fruits may have a high rate of moisture after drying. This means that the consumer is buying at a high rate of cost. When natural dried fruits have a high percentage of moisture, they tend to encourage the growth of molds and fungi.

Last, but not least, the naturally dried fruits tend to collect dust during the drying process. Therefore, the natural dried fruits and vegetables are not the best in quality. They would be of poorer quality. Unfortunately, the natural health food stores charge the consumers very high prices. Many times, the food they sell is as good as those in the food stores and sometimes better or worse, depending upon the method of processing and preparation.

As far as the natural vitamins they sell, it is impossible for any store anywhere in the world to sell natural vitamins. First of all, natural vitamins are found in their natural sources, namely, plants and animals. Most vitamins are synthetic and not natural. No one can afford to sell natural vitamins; otherwise, the whole country of the U.S. should be converted into a farmland to extract vitamins from their natural sources.

The natural health food stores do sell synthetic vitamins under the definition of "Natural." Consumers have to realize this; otherwise, they are paying too much money for the synthetic vitamins under the pretext of being "Natural."

D. **Concerns of the Author.** The author of this book has been in North America since 1962. He has worked and established many centers, societies and organizations. He established contacts with Muslim countries. He started writing in his field since then. His writings were mainly in English and Arabic. Some of his writings were translated to some Muslim languages for the benefit of Muslims in their homelands. Some of his writings were mainly in the field of Daʻwah, Friday Khutab, and introducing Islam, while other writings were in the field of food, health and behavior. At the end of this book there is a list of his publications. They consist mainly of books and booklets, and they can be obtained from the publisher.[4]

The author, along with other Muslim friends, got together and expressed their concerns about the chaos. Finally, they organized and founded a professional society to deal with the problem. This society is called Islamic Food and Nutrition Council of America (IFANCA).[5]

E. **IFANCA's Concerns.** As students of Shari'ah and of science and technology, we were concerned not to leave the Muslims in vacuum. We organized a professional organization in the field of Halal food called: **Islamic Food and Nutrition Council of America (IFANCA).** Some of the leading figures of IFANCA are knowledgeable in Shari'ah only, while some others are experts in the field of food and nutrition sciences. Others are versed in both the Shari'ah and the science of food and nutrition. A combination of all these groups made it possible to work together amicably for a good cause.

This council took upon itself the responsibility to educate the Muslims about the legality and procedures of the slaughtering processes in North America. They also tried to educate the Muslims

---

Foundation for Islamic Knowledge, P.O. Box 665, Lombard, IL 60148.
Fax (708) 627-8894 or Phone (708) 495-4817

IFANCA, P.O. Box 425, Bedford, IL 60499.
Fax (708) 233-1071 or Phone (708)233-1001

about the Shari'ah. A newsletter (The Islamic Perspective) was initiated, and a textbook on "Islamic Dietary Laws and Practices" was published. Seminars and workshops were conducted. Communication with USDA, with Rabbis and some Christian denominations were established. Communications with the American industries were established. All these activities were done for the purpose of establishing Halal foods in America.

Since the Muslim world and their populations are importing foods and meat from America, communications were established with the Muslim world through their embassies, their local Chambers of Commerce, their Department of Commerce and Industries, as well as through their local newspapers, journals and magazines.

Certification for Halal meat was established as well as Certification of Halal ingredients. More information about the activities, services, and achievements of the Council are to be obtained from the IFANCA address directly.

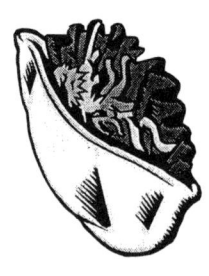

III
HALAL AND HARAM DEFINED

The concepts of Halal and Haram in Islam are very important in the life of every practicing Muslim. In this chapter, these concepts are defined, explained and correlated to foods, diets, and nutrition. The concepts of *Mash-booh* (suspected), *Makrooh* (discouraged or hated) and *Zabiha* (slaughtering according to Islamic laws) are also included.

A.　Halal.　　Halal is an Arabic word which means allowed or lawful. In the case of diets and foods, most of them are considered to be Halal unless they are specified or mentioned in the Qur'an or Hadith (sayings of Prophet Muhammad (pbuh)). Human beings cannot change the unlawful (*Haram*) into lawful (*Halal*). It is also unlawful to make the lawful as unlawful.

The other name of Halal meat would be Zabiha. Please refer to "*Zabiha*" at the end of this chapter. The word "*Halal*" is a Qur'anic term and is used several times in different concepts. Some of them are related to foods. In this respect, Allah (swt) says the following about Halal foods in the Qur'an in Surah Al-Ma'idah (The

Table Spread):

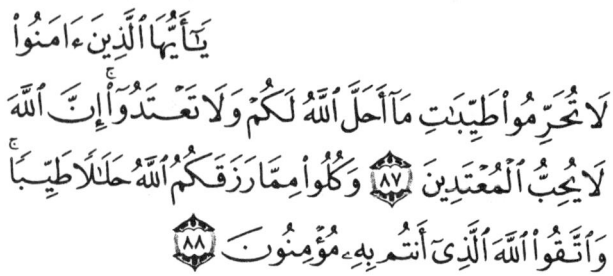

O you who believe! forbid not the good things which Allah (swt) made 'lawful' for you, and transgress not. Lo! Allah (swt) loves not transgressors. Eat of that which Allah (swt) has bestowed on you as food 'lawful' and good, and keep your duty to Allah in Whom you are believers. [5:87-88]

B. Haram. Haram is an Arabic word which, in general, means prohibited or unlawful. In Islam, Haram foods are meant unlawful. They are:

1. Pork and its by-products
2. Alcohol
3. Meat of dead animals
4. Animals slaughtered in a name other than Allah (God (swt)
5. Blood
6. Intoxicating drugs, etc.

If a Muslim uses any of the above listed Haram products, he would be sinful.

In some exceptional cases a Muslim may use the Haram foods in the following circumstances:

1. By mistake, or
2. If he is in danger.

When there is no other food available except the one which is Haram, then he is given the permission to use it to survive only. In this respect Allah (swt) says the following in the Qur'an in Surah Al-Baqarah (The Cow):

$$\text{إِنَّمَا حَرَّمَ عَلَيْكُمُ ٱلْمَيْتَةَ وَٱلدَّمَ وَلَحْمَ ٱلْخِنزِيرِ وَمَا أُهِلَّ بِهِۦ لِغَيْرِ ٱللَّهِ فَمَنِ ٱضْطُرَّ غَيْرَ بَاغٍ وَلَا عَادٍ فَلَا إِثْمَ عَلَيْهِ إِنَّ ٱللَّهَ غَفُورٌ رَّحِيمٌ ۝}$$

He has only forbidden you dead meat, and the flesh of swine and that which any other name hath been invoked besides that of God. But if one is forced by necessity, without willful disobedience nor transgressing due limit, then he is guiltless. For God is Oft-forgiving, Most Merciful. [2:173]

C. **Mash-booh (Shubha).** Mash-booh is an Arabic word which means 'Suspected.' Some items are suspected because a person may not know whether they are Halal or Haram. If there is no written statement in the Qur'an and Hadith about a matter being Halal or Haram, then a person tries his best to make his own judgement and decision. When such a decision is based on the application or on the understanding of the original statement, one may be lead to a degree of suspicion. This is called *Mash-booh*, *Shubha*, or *Mashcook*.

A practicing Muslim prevents himself from being involved in things that are considered Shubha. The concept of preventing oneself is based on the Hadith where Al-Nu'man Ibn Bashir (R) narrated that Prophet Muhammad (pbuh) said:

١٠٨٨ - عن النعمان بن بشير رضي الله عنهما قال: سمعت رسول الله صلى الله عليه وسلم يقول: « إن الحلال بين، وإن الحرام بين، وبينهما مشتبهات لا يعلمهن كثير من الناس، فمن اتقى الشبهات، استبرأ لدينه وعرضه، ومن وقع في الشبهات، وقع في الحرام، كالراعي يرعى حول الحمى يوشك أن يرتع فيه، ألا وإن لكل ملك حمى، ألا وإن حمى الله محارمه، ألا وإن في الجسد مضغة إذا صلحت صلح الجسد كله، وإذا فسدت فسد الجسد كله: ألا وهي القلب » متفق عليه. ورواه من طرق بألفاظ متقاربة.

Halal (Lawful) is clear and Haram (Prohibited) is clear; in between these two are certain things that are suspected (Shubha). Many people may not know whether those items are Halal or Haram. Whosoever, leaves them, he is innocent towards his religion and his conscience. He is, therefore, safe.

Anyone who gets involved in any of these suspected items, he may fall into the unlawful and the prohibition. This case is similar to the one who wishes to raise his animals next to a restricted area, he may step into it. Indeed the restrictions of Allah (swt) are the unlawful (Haram.) ---Agreed Upon---

D. <u>Makrooh.</u> Makrooh is an Arabic word and it means religiously 'discouraged' or 'hated.' In the case of the food industry, any food or diet which is not recommended to eat or drink could be suspected. If through the process of verification, one finds a record of information which is distasteful or harmful (food or drink) to the individual's health, then the food is said to be 'Makrooh' (hated or discouraged). This concept of 'Makrooh' is used in Islamic jurisprudence for any food, liquid, or smoking which is disguised or harmful to the body physically, psychologically, mentally, or spiritually. The person who involves himself in the 'Makrooh' will be blamed on the Day of Judgment.

A person should, therefore, avoid any 'Makrooh' products such as: stimulants, depressants, drug dependencies, smoking, coffee, tea, soft drinks (because of caffeine), garlic and onions on Fridays (because of smell), etc.

E. **Zabiha (Zabeeha).** Zabiha is an Arabic word which, in general means, 'slaughtered.' When an animal is slaughtered according to the teachings of Islam, the meat is considered zabiha. Anytime the word zabiha is used for meat, it should mean Halal meat or lawful meat.

Muslim minorities such as those in North America are requested to make arrangements for slaughtering animals so that the meat will be lawful for them to be eaten. If it is difficult due to the absence of a Muslim community, then an individual Muslim may eat the meat of the "People of the Book" by saying the name of Allah (swt) before eating. This verdict is taken from some schools of thought especially that of Shafiites.

It is reported in the Arabic book of Syed Sabiq "Fiqhus - Sunnah" Chapter of "Meat of the people of the Book," page 298: The meat of the slaughtered animals by Christians or Jews is Halal for Muslims. In this respect, he quotes the verse in Surah Al-Ma'idah (The Table Spread):

ٱلْيَوْمَ أُحِلَّ لَكُمُ ٱلطَّيِّبَٰتُ ۖ وَطَعَامُ ٱلَّذِينَ أُوتُوا۟ ٱلْكِتَٰبَ حِلٌّ لَّكُمْ وَطَعَامُكُمْ حِلٌّ لَّهُمْ ۖ وَٱلْمُحْصَنَٰتُ مِنَ ٱلْمُؤْمِنَٰتِ وَٱلْمُحْصَنَٰتُ مِنَ ٱلَّذِينَ أُوتُوا۟ ٱلْكِتَٰبَ مِن قَبْلِكُمْ إِذَآ ءَاتَيْتُمُوهُنَّ أُجُورَهُنَّ مُحْصِنِينَ غَيْرَ مُسَٰفِحِينَ وَلَا مُتَّخِذِىٓ أَخْدَانٍ ۗ وَمَن يَكْفُرْ بِٱلْإِيمَٰنِ فَقَدْ حَبِطَ عَمَلُهُۥ وَهُوَ فِى ٱلْءَاخِرَةِ مِنَ ٱلْخَٰسِرِينَ ۝

This day are (all) good things made lawful for you. The food of those who have received the Scripture is lawful for you, and your food is lawful for them...
[5:5]

If a name other than Allah (swt) has been mentioned, then there are two opinions about it: One opinion says that the meat slaughtered is considered to be Halal or Zabiha because it is slaughtered by a Christian or a Jew. Allah (swt) knows what they say and He allows us to eat the meat slaughtered by them. This opinion is agreed upon by Ata', Qasim bin Mukhaimarah, Zahri, Rabee'ah, Sha'bi, and Mak'hool.

The other opinion states that if a name other than Allah (swt) has been mentioned at the time of slaughtering, then the meat is Haram (unlawful) for Muslims to eat. This opinion is supported by 'Ali, Aisha, Son of 'Umar, Abi Darda' and Ibadah bin Samit. Their opinions are based upon the meaning of the verse in Surah Al-An'am (The Cattle):

وَلَا تَأْكُلُوا مِمَّا لَمْ يُذْكَرِ اسْمُ اللَّهِ عَلَيْهِ وَإِنَّهُ لَفِسْقٌ وَإِنَّ الشَّيَاطِينَ لَيُوحُونَ إِلَىٰ أَوْلِيَآئِهِمْ لِيُجَٰدِلُوكُمْ وَإِنْ أَطَعْتُمُوهُمْ إِنَّكُمْ لَمُشْرِكُونَ ﴿١٢١﴾

And eat not of that (meats) whereon Allah's name has not been pronounced: that would be impiety. But the Satans ever inspire their friends to contend with you if you were to obey them, you would indeed be Pagans. [6:121]

The consumers are encouraged to look for zabiha meat, and they are to be sure that the slaughtered animals (beef and chickens) were not given the female sex hormone diethyl stilbesterol (DES). The latter has negative effects on the sex behavior of male human beings. As far as the meat of goat and lamb are concerned, there is no proof that such a hormone is added to the animals.

IV
GENERAL CONCEPTS

1. Everything in Islam is Halal unless it is mentioned in Qur'an and /or Hadith to be Haram.
2. The Legislator of Halal and Haram is Allah and Allah alone
3. Changing the Halal to Haram, and the Haram to Halal is a matter of Shirk.
4. Anything that is conducive to Haram is Haram
5. Anything that is doubtful is to be avoided
6. Haram is prohibited to everyone, Muslims and non-Muslims
7. Necessity dictates exceptions
8. Whatever is Halal is good for health; and whatever is bad for health is or should be Haram.
9. You are what you eat -- your health and your personality are affected by the food you eat.
10. Certain foods were recommended because of their healing effects or of their good benefits.
11. Some foods and drinks were prohibited because of their harmful effects on health.
12. The concept of prevention is one of the cardinal principles in

Islam.

13. The concept of purification and detoxification are regularized in Islam through fasting.

14. Eating habits have been laid down through the Prophet's life for a better health and a happy life.

15. Feasts, festivities and special occasions are made to enjoy life as individuals, as families, and as a community.

16. Moderation is endorsed and mandated as a habit in life to enjoy good health.

17. The factors affecting the health and behavior of the individual are:

    a. Genetics and heredity
    b. Foods, nutrition, and eating habits
    c. Society and environment
    d. Guidance of the Supreme Creator
    e. Physical activities
    f. Diseases

V
FALLACIES AND FACTS

A. **Muslim Foods.** Many non-Muslim institutions do not know yet what is a Muslim meal. These institutions could be hospitals, airlines, universities, restaurants, prisons, government agencies, etc. Some non-Muslims do think that a Muslim food may mean Kosher, while others think it is vegetarian. Still another group think it is without pork but may contain ham, lard, or bacon. The more educated ones are those who think that Muslims are not to eat shell fish, clam, lobster, shrimp, crab or whale meat.

As one may see, there is a rainbow of misunderstanding about what a Muslim food is. This type of confusion has started with a good intention of those Muslims who gave such information to the non-Muslims. They based their answers according to their customs, habits, traditions, or according to their personal understanding of their schools of thought. The non-Muslims ended up with a state of confusion. Hence, whenever they want to prepare a menu, each institution had its guidelines according to the information given to the administration of such institution.

There is a great desire for someone to write a booklet on this subject from the Islamic point of view. The writer has to take into consideration the commonalities among the schools of thought. The writer should also give general information and specific ones. He is to give specific menus along with the theoretical and specific ones. These menus should be designed for hospitals, airlines, restaurants, school cafeterias, and so on. A partial list of bonafide catering houses for Halal recipes and menus should also be included too.

A Muslim food therefore, is the one that should meet the following requirements: As far as **Land Animals** are concerned, the following is a list of requirements:

1. The animals should be among those that Allah made them Halal for human consumption. Some of the famous ones are: Cattle, sheep, chickens, goats, camels, gazelles, etc.
2. The feed given to animals should be Halal. In case hog meals were given to these animals in any form, the animals are not Halal to be consumed. The animals have to be isolated for forty (40) days from such feed before they are to be slaughtered.
3. No hormones of any form are to be given to the animals, mainly diethylstilbestrol (DES) and estrogen (EST), etc.
4. The slaughtering should be done by a righteous and a practicing Muslim. The name of Allah should be mentioned such as **Bismillah, Allahu Akbar.** Slaughtering should be with a sharp knife using one slit between the two jugular veins and the wind pipe. The animal should not feel the pain if the process is done fast with a sharp knife. Blood has to be

drained completely before any processing technique is to be done. The Qur'an explicitly demands from the Muslims to eat from those Halal animals that are slaughtered in the name of Allah (swt). If and when an animal is slaughtered in names other than Allah (swt), then that Halal animal will <u>NOT</u> be Halal for Muslims anymore. In that respect, Allah (swt) says in the Qur'an in Surah Al-An'am (The Cattle) the following:

وَلَا تَأْكُلُوا مِمَّا لَمْ يُذْكَرِ اسْمُ اللَّهِ عَلَيْهِ وَإِنَّهُ لَفِسْقٌ وَإِنَّ الشَّيَاطِينَ لَيُوحُونَ إِلَىٰٓ أَوْلِيَآئِهِمْ لِيُجَٰدِلُوكُمْ وَإِنْ أَطَعْتُمُوهُمْ إِنَّكُمْ لَمُشْرِكُونَ ۝

Eat not of (meats) on which Allah's (swt) name has not been pronounced: That would be impiety. but the Satans ever inspire their friends to contend with you if you were to obey them, you would indeed be pagans. [6:121]

5. No chemical preservatives or coloring materials are to be added to the meat while the meat is displayed in the market or even if it is processed in the form of hot dogs, hamburger, etc.

B. <u>Zabiha and Halal.</u> It is usually said that a bonafide animal slaughtered by a Muslim is Halal. Since it is Zabiha, therefore, it should be Halal. It is not necessarily true. Chickens and steers are given a growth hormone called Diethyl Stilbestrol (DES). The latter is given to chickens in their water or as drops in their nostrils, while steers receive it as a pallet behind their ears. DES is a female sex hormone. It is given to increase the size, height, and weight of the animal in a short period of time. Therefore, it is a money making venture.

However, this compound DES, is a steroid hormone, and is resistant to cooking procedures. It is to be transferred to the human body and affects the young men. It can change their masculine feelings to female feelings. Hence their sexual appetite would be toward other males.

Similarly, one has to be careful whether the cows have received the female hormone estrogen (EST) or not. On February 1994, FDA gave the permission to the farmers to use EST on the cows. The hormone after being injected, will increase the size of the milk bladders. Hence, it will also increase the secretion of the milk. This means that more production of milk and more money. The thing that one should worry about is the following fact: Feeding such milk to infants, babies and children may increase their breast after they reach the age of puberty. Boys and girls will have breasts, and they may look Unisex!!..

Finally, not every Zabiha should be considered Halal unless the feed is Halal, the animal is Halal, the process of slaughtering is Halal and the name of Allah is pronounced during the process of slaughtering.

C. Slaughtering Animals. Many confusions are in the minds of Muslims and non-Muslims as to the method of slaughtering. Some claim that butchers suffocate chickens and hence blood stays within the animals. Others claim that cattle are shot by bullets and after they die, the butchers try to slaughter the animals. Other groups claim that the animals are slaughtered through the wind-pipe only without the jugular veins. Some more confusion in this regard is that Rabbis read the name of Allah while the animals are being slaughtered.

All of these are claims without proof. The truth of the matter is that the USDA has rules and regulations about slaughtering of animals. Some of such rules that pertain to Muslim concerns would be:

1.   Chickens: They are put in funnel upside down and an electric knife with circular blade is to cut-off the head from the neck completely. The animal is to drain its blood while still hanging in the funnel. Then transferred to hot bathing of water to facilitate the removal of the feather and to let most of the blood to bleed out.

2.   Cattle: Cattle are zoomed in an alley. An electric battery is to hit the head so that the animal is knocked down unconscious. While being in that state, it is lifted up and slaughtered by a knife. The butcher cuts the wind-pipe and the two jugular veins.

While being lifted upside down the blood drains. It is transferred on conveyors. Later the head is removed and the viscera as well. Finally, the skin is removed, cleaned and processed.

However, wild animals in the farm cannot be caught easily. The farmers may shoot the animals before slaughtering them. Therefore, slaughtering does follow shooting. However, wild animals are the exception for their consumption by the consumers.

D.   Kosher Foods.   Many Muslims feel that every Kosher food should be Halal. This is not true. Some Kosher foods do contain alcohol which is prohibited in Islam. Kosher gelatin may contain pork products and still it is Kosher for the Jews. Gelatin is deficient in tryptophan as an essential amino acid. Plants are also deficient in the same component. USDA considers it to be similar and/or equal to plant proteins. Hence, Jews consider it to be Kosher. To the Muslims Kosher gelatin is <u>not</u> Halal.   Kosher meats (chickens and beef) may also contain the female hormones DES or EST. Both are dangerous to the health of people. Kosher meats may also contain Sodium Nitrate-Nitrite as well. Both are also dangerous to the health of the consumers. Therefore, one has to be careful when he says that Kosher foods are Halal.. Some of the followers of the school of Hanafi believe that Kosher meat is Halal, while the meat of the People of the Book is not. Their understanding is that Rabbis do slaughter animals in the name of Allah. This is not true. Other

Muslims do believe that Jews are part of the People of the Book, while the Christians are not. This not true at all. Both Christians and Jews are called People of the Book. Their faith of today is the same as it was when the Qur'an was revealed to Prophet Muhammad (pbuh).

Muslims of today do constitute a big community in the non-Muslim world. As long as Muslims are a community, as long as they have mosques, and as long as they are well established, they are obliged to make sure that their foods and liquids are all Halal. This means that they have to prepare these foods and liquids by themselves, or they have to supervise the non-Muslim industries to prepare Halal foods and liquids. They are <u>not</u> to rely on Kosher or foods of the "People of the Book" daily for the rest of their lives.

Muslim governments are obligated by laws of Allah, to make sure that they are to produce Halal foods; and in case they are to import them, that the foods and liquids are all Halal.

E. **Supermarket Meats.** Some Muslims do consider the meat of the American market is Halal because the animals are slaughtered by either Christians or Jews. The latter groups are considered People of the Book (Ahl-Kitab). Such group of Muslims have considered the concepts of Halal/Haram from a spiritual point of view. However, they should also consider the ideas of Halal/Haram from the health point of view.

The American meat business people do spray the meat with

sodium nitrate in combination with sodium nitrite. These two chemicals produce nitrous acid which in turn reacts with the amine group of the protein of the meat to produce nitrosoamine. This chemical compound produces a red pigment on the meat, which turns the color of the meat red. A customer may think that the meat is fresh, red and tender. However, these chemicals do produce cancer in people who eat such type of meat. Hence, the meat of the market (chicken and beef) should not be considered Halal from the health point of view. Meat of the market may have also the hormones DES or EST. Both are dangerous to the health of the consumers. However, goats and lambs do not fall into this category because the farmers do not use the growth hormone for them.

F.   Vegetarian Foods.   Many concerned Muslims think that vegetarian foods could be the safest to eat. Their assumption is that it does not contain meat of any variety. Accordingly there should not be any problem regarding Halal/Haram or even Zabiha. In reality, this is not true. Vegetarian foods may contain alcohol. The latter is not Haram to the vegetarian people. Therefore, Muslims should be concerned if they wish to eat vegetarian foods. Moreover, one should recognize that there are many varieties of vegetarian foods: fruitarian, ovo-vegetarian, lacto-vegetarian, ovo-lacto-vegetarian, and a combination of others. A Muslim should be educated about each and every variety of such vegetarian foods. At the same time, he should be concerned about the concept of a well-balanced diet. Some of the vegetables and fruits are deficient in lysine, methionine, threonine, iron, or other essential nutrients. Hence, one may end up with health complication.

G.   **Sea foods.**   Sea animals as a source of food have been and are still an issue among Muslims. The school of Ja'fari has many restrictions about the lawfulness of the sea animals as a source of food. However, the Ahlis-Sunnah Wal-Jama'at have more leniency toward those fishes. But still there are some differences among them, too. The school of Hanafi is more strict while the other three schools admonish the lawfulness of all types of varieties of sea animals without any exceptions. The Qur'an is very clear when Allah (swt) says in Surah Al-Ma'idah (Table Spread) the following:

أُحِلَّ لَكُمْ صَيْدُ ٱلْبَحْرِ وَطَعَامُهُۥ مَتَٰعًا لَّكُمْ وَلِلسَّيَّارَةِۖ وَحُرِّمَ عَلَيْكُمْ صَيْدُ ٱلْبَرِّ مَا دُمْتُمْ حُرُمًاۗ وَٱتَّقُواْ ٱللَّهَ ٱلَّذِىٓ إِلَيْهِ تُحْشَرُونَ ۝٩٦

Lawful to you is the pursuit of fishing and its use for food, - for the benefit of yourselves and those who travel; but forbidden is the pursuit of land-game: - As long as you are in the Sacred Precincts or in the state of pilgrimage and fear Allah, to whom you shall be gathered back. [5:96]

The confusion starts when there are groups of heterogeneous Muslims residing in a non-Muslim country, and belonging themselves to different schools of thought. This type of confusion is augmented when the majority of those Muslims are ignorant of the teachings of their own schools.

The most disturbing situation is when Muslims accuse other Muslims because they follow other schools of thought. Muslims have to learn how to be knowledgeable, wise, amiable, friendly, and open-minded.

H. **Choosing Wrong Food Products.** The title reflects the unbelievable information. Every human being tries to choose the right food products for good health. People choose the right food items and the right liquids so that they can stay healthy, strong and happy.

For Muslims it is more so, as they are instructed in the Qur'an and the Hadith, that they should select the best. In order to live healthy, they should listen to the instructions of Allah and His Messenger. Muslims should eat what is Halal, and refrain form what is Haram, Makrooh, Mashbooh, or even distasteful.

Allah demanded from His Messengers to eat from the good and lawful foods. In Surah Al-Mu'minoon (The Believers), Allah (swt) says the following:

بِسْمِ اللَّهِ ﴿يَا أَيُّهَا الرُّسُلُ كُلُوا مِنَ الطَّيِّبَاتِ وَاعْمَلُوا صَالِحًا ۖ إِنِّي بِمَا تَعْمَلُونَ عَلِيمٌ﴾

O you messengers! Eat of the good things, and do right. Lo! I am aware of what you do. [23:51]

Allah also demanded from the believers to do the same. In Surah Al-Baqarah (The Cow) Allah says the following:

﴿يَا أَيُّهَا الَّذِينَ آمَنُوا كُلُوا مِنْ طَيِّبَاتِ مَا رَزَقْنَاكُمْ وَاشْكُرُوا لِلَّهِ إِنْ كُنْتُمْ إِيَّاهُ تَعْبُدُونَ﴾ ﴿١٧٢﴾

O you who believe! Eat of the good things wherewith We have provided you, and render thanks to Allah if it is (indeed) He Whom you worship. [2:172]

It should be stated here that one of the People of the Cave was asked to go to the market and buy the best and the most delicious food. The Qur'an states the following in Surah Al-Kahf (The Cave):

﴿فَابْعَثُوا أَحَدَكُمْ بِوَرِقِكُمْ هَٰذِهِ إِلَى الْمَدِينَةِ فَلْيَنْظُرْ أَيُّهَا أَزْكَىٰ طَعَامًا فَلْيَأْتِكُمْ بِرِزْقٍ مِنْهُ وَلْيَتَلَطَّفْ وَلَا يُشْعِرَنَّ بِكُمْ أَحَدًا﴾ ﴿١٩﴾

Now send you then one of you with this money of yours to the town: Let him find out which is the best food (to be had) and bring some to you, (that you may satisfy your hunger therewith) and let him behave with care and courtesy, and let him not inform any one about you. **[18:19]**

Muslims are demanded to shun away from imitating the non-Muslims even in their dress, behaviors, manners, attire, and outlook. They are even instructed, while making *Du'a'* to be selective in the use of certain words or expressions. Allah instructed the Muslims while making *Du'a'*, not to use the word *Ra'ina*, but to use the word *Unzurna*. The first word has a negative connotation while the latter has the right appeal and request. In Surah Al-Baqarah (the Cow), Allah says the following:

يَٰٓأَيُّهَا ٱلَّذِينَ ءَامَنُواْ لَا تَقُولُواْ رَٰعِنَا وَقُولُواْ ٱنظُرْنَا وَٱسْمَعُواْ وَلِلْكَٰفِرِينَ عَذَابٌ أَلِيمٌ ۝

O you of Faith! Say not (to the prophet) Ra'ina, but say Unzurna and hearken (to Him): To those without Faith is a grievous punishment. **[2:104]**

However, in Surah Al-Nisa' (The Women) Allah informed the Muslims not to repeat the same mistake of previous groups of people.

One such a case is the information about the children of Israel. The Qur'an states the following:

$$\text{مِّنَ ٱلَّذِينَ هَادُواْ يُحَرِّفُونَ ٱلْكَلِمَ عَن مَّوَاضِعِهِۦ وَيَقُولُونَ سَمِعْنَا وَعَصَيْنَا وَٱسْمَعْ غَيْرَ مُسْمَعٍ وَرَٰعِنَا لَيًّا بِأَلْسِنَتِهِمْ وَطَعْنًا فِى ٱلدِّينِ ۚ وَلَوْ أَنَّهُمْ قَالُواْ سَمِعْنَا وَأَطَعْنَا وَٱسْمَعْ وَٱنظُرْنَا لَكَانَ خَيْرًا لَّهُمْ وَأَقْوَمَ وَلَٰكِن لَّعَنَهُمُ ٱللَّهُ بِكُفْرِهِمْ فَلَا يُؤْمِنُونَ إِلَّا قَلِيلًا ۝}$$

***Of the Jews there are those who displace words from their (right) places, and say: "We hear and we disobey." And "Here, may you not hear," and Ra'ina with a twist of their tongues and a slander to Faith. If only they had said, " We hear and we obey." And "Do hear." And " Do look at us." It would have been better for them, and more proper. But Allah has cursed them for their unbelief; and but few of them will believe.* [4:46]**

Unfortunately, there are some Muslims in different parts of the world who want to imitate the non-Muslims and to obtain everything from them. There are some Muslim countries that are importing the wrong foods and drinks under false names. They import non-alcoholic beer, wine, vodka, whiskey, champagne, etc. They import beef bacon. Lard, turkey ham, etc. The non-alcoholic drinks have by law 0.5% alcohol.

Do these Muslims have to import such products that have their own definitions, connotations and understanding? Do these Muslims want to imitate the West in the Haram products, so that they will be called civilized, modernized, liberated, and good friends to the non-Muslims? Don't these Muslims recognize that Islamic teachings instruct them not to imitate the non-Muslims; otherwise, they will be gathered on the Day of Judgement with them?!

The Muslim world has all types of fresh juices and fresh drinks in their lands. If they want processed beverages, they can have them too. If they want to use different wordings, terminologies or definitions they can do it . Their Arabic language is rich in terminologies, definitions and expressions. There are 10,000 words of Arabic origin in the English language, and 100,000 words in the Spanish language. They can use from these words the ones that reflect their identity, as well as the Halal methods, products and even the words.

VI
STRATEGIES FOR BETTER HEALTH

A. <u>General.</u> Everyone has to eat daily, but a good number of the consumers may not know what to eat for a better health. They may buy whatever is available or is cheaper. Some foods could be of lower quality than others, and most foods are preserved with chemical additives, coloring materials, flavoring extracts, etc. Alternatives are proposed to the consumers so that they will be given the chance to choose, select and reject. There is nothing called absolute good or bad. One has to realize that certain aspects in food preservation are better than others. Hence, one has to choose the best alternatives available for a better nutritive value, a better biological value and finally for a better health.

The alternatives are designed to help the consumers to eat, drink, and live a happy life. The life of the individual is very precious in the sight of Allah. The author is, then, keen to protect the rights of the consumers, to respect them, to dignify them, and to help them live with honor, dignity, and happiness. In so doing, one has to try the best to please Allah and satisfy one's conscience. This section is divided into categories: (b) beware and (c) alternatives.

B.   Beware.   The items under this category could be unlawful (Haram), objectionable (Makrooh), suspected (Mash-booh), of poor nutritive value or may cause some health hazards. The consumers are requested to be aware of the side effects of the following:

1. Pork, lard, bacon and ham.
2. Shortening in general and animal shortening in particular
3. Artificial sweeteners --   saccharin, etc.
4. Alcoholic beverages
5. Non-alcoholic beverages: Coca-Cola and Pepsi-Cola, Seven-Up, all sodas, cider, etc.
6. Chemical preservatives including nitrates-nitrites.
7. Synthetic coloring materials.
8. Synthetic flavoring extracts.
9. All types of stimulus products including coffee and tea.
10. Gelatinous capsules and the coating materials for drugs and vitamins.
11. Intoxicating and addicting drugs.
12. Gelatins and animal jell.
13. Soft water and/or water softening agents.
14. Refined products.
15. Any animals products unless the consumers is aware of the natural source
16. Any types of hormones including DES, pork insulin, and EST.

17. Glycerides: mono- and Di-glyceride (unless they are vegetables).
18. Enzymes including rennin (rennet), pepsin of pork origin.
19. Brewers' yeast because the source is the brewing of beer.

C. Alternatives. The items under this category are designed according to the teachings of Islam, the science of nutrition and the health of the individuals. The consumers are encouraged to include the following in their daily food habits.

1. Include vegetables in every meal
2. Use fresh fruits as desserts instead of cakes or pies.
3. Use fresh juices instead of preserved ones. Fresh juices are even better than soft drink
4. Use herbal teas instead of coffee and tea.
5. Fresh foods are better than frozen foods. The latter ones are better than canned foods. Finally, canned foods are even better than dried foods.
6. Freeze-dried foods are of highly quality foods.
7. Use raw vegetable oils (liquid) instead of fats or hydrogenated vegetable oils (solid).
8. Pressure cooking method is better than the normal cooking.
9. The use of microwave oven is nutritionally a very good method
10. Look for spring water, mountain natural water and even hard

water instead of soft water.
11. Whenever possible, use honey instead of sugar and use brown instead of white sugar.
12. Use whole cereal grains instead of the refined ones.
13. Used brown breads instead of the white ones.
14. Use whole flour instead of the bleached one.
15. Use brown rice instead of the polished (white)one.
16. Look for "Zabiha" meat and Zabiha products in all foods.
17. Use plant jell (Agar) instead of the animals ones.
18. Use microbial yeast instead of brewer's yeast.
19. Look for microbial or plant enzymes instead of the animal ones. Animal enzymes could be: Pepsin, Rennin or Rennet.
20. Look for natural flavorings, colorings, preservatives instead of the synthetic ones. The source should be plant.

VII
IMPROVING FOOD VALUES

For the sake of getting high nutritive value (NV) and biological value (BV) of food at a low cost, the following recommendations are suggested:

1. Reduce consumption of meat, as it is expensive.
2. Use mixed vegetables at a time.
3. Use milk with cereals and other plant food at meals.
4. Use plain yogurt daily in your diet, as it improves the BV, GI (gastrointestinal) microfilaria, and reduces gas in the stomach.
5. Use eggs as a source of protein. Don't worry much about cholesterol, as the quantity you eat is not much to worry about. The presence of lecithin in egg yolk helps to mobilize cholesterol in the body. The presence of biotin in egg yolk is the best source in nature.
6. Fish is cheaper than beef. It has high BV for its proteins, and the fats have a high concentration of PUFA (poly-unsaturated fatty acids) that are best for good health.
7. Chicken is cheaper than beef. It has good NV for its protein and have better quality of fats and oils than beef. Try to peel

off the skin as it has saturated fats and high cholesterol.

8. Fresh fruit salad is very good to have daily as it supplies vitamins, minerals, essential amino acids, and some essential oils. They help digestion and reduce cholesterol.

9. For those who drink soft drinks, coffee and tea, they are requested to eat peanuts as it has a high concentration of magnesium (Mg), while the soft drinks deplete the body from the electrolytes and especially magnesium and potassium (Mg and K), which are essential for the heart rhythms.

10. Use honey instead of sugar as the first does contain amino acids, minerals, vitamins and other useful sugars. Honey has high content of fructose. It needs less insulin than glucose for metabolism.

11. A high concentration of Vitamin D mobilizes calcium (Ca) from bones into the blood stream and deposits the calcium into soft tissues. Hence, one has to be aware of it.

12. Use natural Halal foods as a source of natural vitamins.

13. Stop smoking as it consumes 70 mg of Vitamin C per cigarette. Smoking causes lung cancer.

14. Stop drinking alcohol as they affect the central nervous system (CNS), heart, brain, red blood cells (RBC), stomach, liver, pancreases, absorption and general metabolism.

15. Drugs do affects stomach microfilaria, thus reducing the BV; even antibiotic do the same.

VIII
RECOMMENDATIONS

Following is a series of recommendations to the consumers, to the food industries, and to the Muslim countries. These recommendations are meant to bridge the gap between the different groups (producers and consumers), so that they will live happily. These recommendations are also good for Muslim countries that are importing foods from every corner of the world. By knowing the true information, less friction occurs, more transactions will take place, and business will flourish.

A. **Consumers.** It is recommended that consumers should:
1. Read labels before buying the food products.
2. Read the ingredients on the food labels and understand the meaning of every ingredient.
3. Read the expiration date of the foods.
4. Recognize the difference between food nutrients and food preservatives.
5. Know the percentages of the nutrients in relation to the US RDA (Recommended Daily Allowance) and not to MDR (Minimum Daily Allowance).
6. Know the sources of each ingredient as well as the sources of

the food preservatives.

7. Recognize that natural flavorings and colorings are better for health than synthetics, especially if the natural source is plant.
8. Ask the food industries and bakeries about any ingredient or preservative that is doubtful.
9. Consult specialists and references before jumping into a wrong conclusion.
10. Muslims are to consult the Qur'an and the Hadith to know which items might be Haram (unlawful), Halal (lawful), Makrooh (objectionable), Mashbooh (suspected), recommended and the like.

B. Food Industries. It is recommended that food industries should:

1. Include on the labels all ingredients, additives, and especially preservatives, as well as the source(s) for every ingredient which is very helpful to the consumers.
2. Offer special foods which are prepared according to Islamic Laws: devoid of any pork (meats and fats or its by- products), and slaughtered in the name of Allah (swt) (God) with a proper method. Special wording should be written on the label: "Halal"meat or "Zabiha" or "according to Islamic Laws," or even "Muslim food."
3. Give more information about these products from an Islamic

perspective in both English and any of the following language: Arabic, Urdu, Persian, Turkish, Swahili, Howsa, Indonesian, or Malaysian, when exporting to the Muslim world.

4. Recruit Muslim consultants for their advice from an Islamic perspective.

C. Muslim Countries.

1. As long as the Muslim countries are importing foods and food products from non-Muslim countries, they have a responsibility to inform the food producers about the rules and regulations in Islam regarding various foods.

2. The Chambers of Commerce in every Muslim country should keep in touch with every food exporter and importer for the same purpose.

3. The Departments of Commerce in Muslim countries should pass along the information about Islam and foods to the Chamber of Commerce in every country exporting foods.

4. The Department of Commerce in the Muslim countries should recruit concerned Muslims whose specialties are in Food Sciences and Technology to seek their advice and recommendations.

5. The Muslim governments should publish, in different languages, booklets, books, pamphlets, brochuress, and other literature about Islam and foods.

6. The Muslim embassies should be more involved in educating the exporting companies as well as the local Muslims about the Islamic requirements for Halal foods.

7. The Muslim countries should sponsor yearly conferences concerning Halal Foods. They should invite Muslim Scholars in these fields as well as Muslim scholars in Islamic Shari'ah. People from different industries should be invited so that they will be informed and be educated.

IX
FINAL REMARKS

Muslims of America are no more isolated from the Muslims of the world. Muslims everywhere can get in touch with one another through phone, fax, Hamm radios, satellite, TV, Internet Computer, and other technological communication facilities. Muslims may be living together in the same area, but they themselves might be of different schools of thought. They are from different nationalities, linguistic and ethnic backgrounds. They have different customs, habits and traditions. Therefore, they are no more isolated but they are integrated. However, they are still a heterogenous group.

Therefore, no one should enforce one's school of thought over the other. Muslims have to find the commonalities among the schools of thought if they wish to live together as a United Muslim Ummah. Muslims should request a large number of 'Ulama' to develop a unified understanding of the Islamic Shari'ah that answers contemporary questions.

Meanwhile, Muslims are to adjust themselves to each other's understanding of the Shari'ah without making any disturbances. They have to realize that their school is not the only one, and it may not be the best one. All are good at their times. They are good now too. But it is the contemporary Muslims who should realize, understand, accommodate and adjust. At the same time, Muslims have to work hard to inform each other across the whole globe about their concerns and the possible solutions, too. They are to bring Halal foods to every corner of the world. It is their responsibility and duty to do so. Halal foods are the healthiest foods, and Muslims have to propagate this message to all the people of the world.

Muslims are unfortunately more towards being consumers than being producers. They import so many things from the non-Muslim countries. Muslims are obliged by Laws of Shari'ah to demand from the producing industries to supply them with Halal foods and drinks. The food industries as well as the pharmaceutical companies are willing to produce what the consumers want. There are more than 1.2 billion Muslims in the world. The producing countries are ready to produce for the Muslims Halal foods, liquids, medicinal drugs, and others. All what is required is to ask and to demand.

On the other hand, the Muslim countries have to start being among the producing and exporting nations rather than being from the consuming nations. Muslims will be respected by all if they try their best to please Allah by following His Revelation in the Qur'an and as explained by Prophet Muhammad (pbuh) through the Hadith and his Sunnah.

To fulfill all these hopes and visions, the Muslim governments have also a duty and a responsibility to enforce only Halal foods and drinks in their own countries. They are to hold a series of seminars, workshops, conferences and conventions in this respect. By doing such activities, a better future is waiting for all.

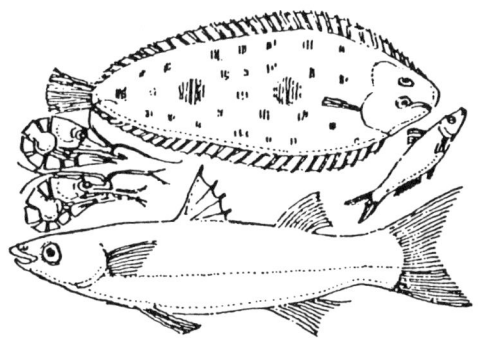

All Marine Animals are Halal

Yusuf Al-Qaradawi stated in his book, The Lawful and the Prohibited, "Marine animals, that is, those which live in water and cannot survive outside it, are all halal. It does not matter in what way they are obtained: whether they are taken out of the water dead or alive, whole or in pieces, whether they are fish or marine animals, whether they are called sea dogs or sea hogs, or whether they are caught by a Muslim or a non-Muslim. The Most Generous Lord has opened wide His bounty upon His servants by permitting them to eat all marine animals, without the requirement of bleeding..." [Al-Qaradawi, The Lawful and the Prohibited, p. 52. Illustration from Premila Lal's book, Indian Cooking for Pleasure, 1970]

ADDENDUM

A. Kosher Gelatin

The following is a statement by the Islamic Food and Nutrition Council of America (IFANCA) published in their newsletter, <u>The Islamic Perspective</u> Vol. (11), No. (1), Pg. (6), 1994, about Kosher Gelatin.

IFANCA frequently receives inquiries about gelatin, especially about Kosher gelatin as present in Jell-O-type desserts, yogurt and many other products. Sometimes gelatin is listed on the product labels but oftentimes there is no mention of it on the labels.

Gelatin is a protein product commercially made from pork skin, cattle bones, calf skin and now from fish skin. In the manufacturing industry there is no distinction made as to the source of gelatin present in the food products.

Most Kosher certifying agencies permit the use of all types of gelatin in Kosher certified products without reference to its origin. They consider gelatin as a neutral (parve) chemical and not a meat ingredient. Hence they seem to have no problem with pork gelatin.

Therefore, the so-called Kosher gelatin might actually be pork gelatin or bone gelatin. According to very reliable sources, the Kosher gelatin is actually made from naturally degreased bones that come from the fields in India and Pakistan. The bones of animals either thrown away by people after eating the meat or from the dead animals stay in the fields or open areas until all remaining pieces of flesh and grease is eaten away by vultures, carnivores, insects, worms and microorganisms. Such bones are collected by scavengers and sold to companies for industrial use to manufacture gelatin and other products.

In 1984, we printed a letter from General Foods, the manufacturer of Jell-O desserts. According to General Foods sources, the information in this letter is still true. General Foods product is certified Kosher. The letter claims that the source of gelatin is ANY animal that has been slaughtered for food purposes. That may be true but it does not exclude pork.

IFANCA is working with several companies to make Halal products available. IFANCA only approves gelatin made from fish and/or halal animals slaughtered by Muslims according to the Islamic law.

Recently the Municipalities of the United Arab Emirates have taken action and banned several products containing gelatin.

B. Ingredients vs. Products

Due to the complexity of tracing the source of various ingredients of which a food or a drink is made up of, many halal conscious Muslim consumers look for a list of grocery items for consumption. A few lists and some books enumerating Halal/Haram status of items for Muslim consumption have been in circulation amongst the Muslims in the USA. While the intention of the compilers of such lists-books cannot be doubted, the fact remains that such lists-books become outdated soon after their publication. The products researched today enjoying the Halal status may change anytime to **Haram** upon the inclusions of one, two, or many Haram ingredients due to formulation change and/or for economic consideration. In absence of any understanding and/or contract with the manufacturer, Haram ingredients find their way into the so-called Halal items without any notice to the Muslim consumers. The manufacturer is obligated to list the name of ingredients of an item on the label. But he is not obligated to include only halal ingredients(s). Thus a product included under Halal category in the list or book today may become **haram** tomorrow and yet Muslims continue to buy and consume such (haram) products (assuming them halal according to the list or book).

There are 5.5 million Jews in the U.S.A., and an estimated 16% Jewish households follow Kosher guidelines. Nonetheless, there are more than 23,000 items that are certified Kosher with Kosher symbol on them for convenience. There are more than 8 million Muslims in the U.S.A. and an estimated 75% of the Muslim households follow Halal guidelines in one form or another. Because the Muslim consumers have failed to exert pressure on the manufacturers, the term Halal is rather unknown, leave alone the compliance of Halal standards. With the ready made list or book of Halal/Haram food items, the manufacturers are getting free promotions (advertisement) of their products without any obligation of compliance with Halal standards. Besides the (halal) status of such product can be changed without any notice and Muslims continue to buy such products still assuming them halal.

Considering the buying power of Muslim food dollars in the U.S.A. (about 10 billion dollars annually), Muslims should speak out to the manufacturers for the compliance of Halal standards. While Islamic Food and Nutrition Council of America developed all the procedures and standards on manufacturers has resulted in a lack of regard for the productions of halal items.

As an intermediary step IFANCA has come up with 'Halal Slide Guide' enumerating the Halal/Haram status of the most commonly used ingredients (not products). This guide enables Muslims to check all the ingredients on the label, determine their Halal/Haram status, and then select the item if all the ingredients are halal. This is a fool-proof device enabling Muslims to make halal selections based on the ingredients which by law are listed on the food package.

For a more permanent solution, Muslim should call and/or write to the manufacturers and insist on producing items complying Halal standards. Manufacturers can be referred to qualified Halal certifying agencies such as IFANCA for Halal certification. The demand and magnitude of Muslim consumers can easily convince manufacturers for halal productions. Once a manufacturer finds a halal market niche and cater to the Muslim consumers with Halal certification and halal symbol, other competitors may follow. Consequently a whole array of Halal products with Halal certification and halal symbol for easy selection will, Insha Allah, be found in the U.S. supermarkets. A concerted effort to promote halal is needed indeed. This is a challenge and an opportunity.

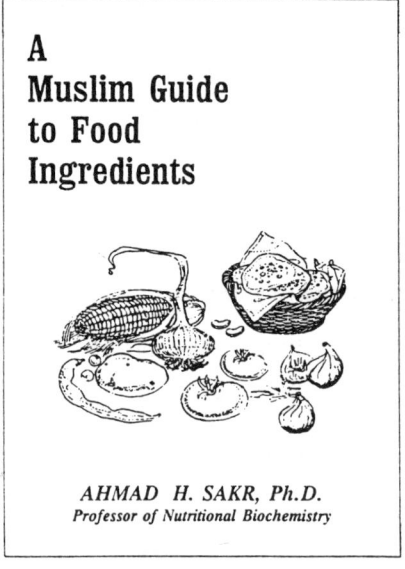

A
Muslim Guide
to Food
Ingredients

AHMAD H. SAKR, Ph.D.
Professor of Nutritional Biochemistry

C. From Haram to Halal

Islam demanded from Muslims to follow, adopt, and practice the Halal (lawful) in their daily life. On the other hand, Islam instructed Muslims to shun away, disdain, and forbid what is Haram (unlawful).

Muslims have no right to change the Haram into Halal for any reason. In as much as they have no right to change Halal into Haram. Muslims have to accept what has been revealed to Prophet Muhammed (pbuh), to practice it, and to live it in its totality.

To live and practice the teachings of Islam, one has to seek the best, and the best is no more than what has been made Halal by Allah (swt).

In a non-Muslim society such as the American society, Muslims cannot jump from Haram to Halal in one step, in a twinkle of an eye. They cannot change the existing infrastructural systems of the un-Islamic society in one day and in one step. To be realistic, they must have the following:

- Sincerity and good intention that they want to live according to the teachings of Islam.
- They have to plan a strategy for moving from Haram to Halal systems.
- They should take the initiative in changing themselves and their un-Islamic habits and customs.

- They should try to apply the teachings of Islam step by step and enrich themselves with the knowledge of Islam.

To go from the lowest level i.e. Haram to the highest level i.e. Halal, one has to realize that it takes time, effort, energy, knowledge, wisdom, money, and the like. Also, one has to realize that he/she can go only one step at a time, otherwise nothing can be changed or improved.

Some of the steps needed to be considered between Haram and Halal are the following:

1. **Haram:** unlawful
2. **Makrooh:** disliked
3. **Mashbooh:** suspected
4. **Ja'iz/Makrooh:** possible with dislike
5. **Ja 'iz/Maqbool:** possible with acceptance
6. **Maqbool:** accepted
7. **Mustahabb:** liked, recommended, or strongly recommended
8. **Halal:** lawful

The step-by-step approach is advisable in all aspects of life, and in every system to be achieved, i.e. religious, social, cultural, economic, educational, industrial, political, legal, judicial, agricultural, and even in the fields of customs, habits, traditions, manners, behaviors, and the like. If an Islamic state has to achieve the Halal in any aspect of life, one has to give those in authority the benefit of the doubt, and know that it takes time, effort, money, and manpower to achieve the Halal.

The concept of the step-by-step might be the wisest idea to be followed in order to reach the highest level of acceptance by Allah (swt), i.e. the Halal that Allah (swt) has prescribed for human beings.

Those who have recently accepted Islam, should realize that they should abandon the un-Islamic customs and habits of their society. However, it takes time to practice, and become familiar with the Islamic instructions; such as *salat* (prayer), *siyam* (fasting), *zakat* (poor-due), *Hajj* (pilgrimage), *Qur'an memorization, Tafseer, Fiqh, Hadith, Seerah, Sharee'ah*, and other aspects of Islam.

Our beloved Prophet (pbuh) informed us to take Islam as an easy way of life, and instructed us to apply it step by step so as to understand and enjoy what we are doing. It was reported by Abu Hurairah that the Prophet (pbuh) said:

٢٦٢ - عن أبي هريرة رضي الله عنه عن النبي صلى الله عليه وسلم قال : « إنَّ الدِّينَ يُسْرٌ ، وَلَنْ يُشَادَّ الدِّينُ إلاَّ غَلَبَهُ ، فَسَدِّدُوا وَقَارِبُوا وَأَبْشِرُوا، وَاسْتَعِينُوا بِالْغَدْوَةِ وَالرَّوْحَةِ وَشَيْءٍ مِنَ الدُّلْجَةِ » رواه البخاري .
وفي رواية له : « سَدِّدُوا وَقَارِبُوا وَاغْدُوا وَرُوحُوا ، وَشَيْءٌ مِنَ الدُّلْجَةِ ، الْقَصْدَ الْقَصْدَ تَبْلُغُوا » .

The religion (of Islam) is indeed easy. Whoever makes it tough is a loser. Hence, follow it with moderation, be close (to it); give glad tidings, follow it in the morning, afternoon, and during the last hours of the night.

It is most important that one takes the initiative and starts with one step at a time. First, he/she should give himself/herself the time to acquire the knowledge, then try to practice what he/she learned. He/she should associate himself/herself with those who are 'Alims (knowledgeable) and those who are sincere in practicing their religion. He/she should be aspiring for the best, and the highest degree in Islam, i.e., the Halal, and the degree of Ihsan.

In so doing, Muslilms will be able to change from Haram to Halal for the love of Allah (swt). Finally, it is left to Allah to help them achieve their aims and objectives. Indeed Allah (swt) will not change the condition of an individual, a group, a community, a nation, or an Ummah, unless they are ready to change themselves. Allah (swt) indeed has said in the Qur'an in Surah Al-Ra'd the following:

إِنَّ ٱللَّهَ لَا يُغَيِّرُ مَا بِقَوْمٍ حَتَّىٰ يُغَيِّرُواْ مَا بِأَنفُسِهِمْ

"Verily never will Allah (swt) change the condition of a people until they change their inner selves" **[13:11]**

The concept of step-by-step should not be misunderstood by saying that I will not start fasting till I finish all matters regarding prayers. Or, I will not perform Hajj till I finish the other pillars of Islam; or, I will not read Hadith till I finish reading the whole Qur'an; or, I will not read anything about Seerah or Fiqh till I finish reading the whole Qur'an or the whole Hadith; or, I will not go to the Friday prayers till I am praying the five daily prayers on time. This is not what is meant by the concept of the step-by-step approach for applying Islam. Islam is a total way of life, and one has to try to apply all its teachings as much as possible, within one's limited capacity, within one's limited understanding, within one's limited situation, and within one's limited threshold.

I hope and pray that Muslims will do their best to apply Islam in their private life, as well as in their public life.   Ameen!

D. List of Halal-Haram Ingredients

The following list of Halal / Haram ingredients and additives is taken from the book (A Muslim Guide to Food Ingredients, by Dr. A. H. Sakr). The symbols used between parentheses are: AL (alcohol), AN (animal origin), H (health reasons), and P (plant origin).

PARTIAL LIST OF CLASSIFIED INGREDIENTS AND ADDITIVES

LAWFUL (HALAL)	SUSPECTED (MASH-BOOH)	UNLAWFUL (HARAM)
ADDITIVES	ADDITIVES	ADDITIVES

Natural: sugar, salt, honey, adipic acid, vinegar, citric acid, black pepper, mustard	Yeast (brewer's) (AL)
	  Sodium nitrate, nitrate (H)
	  Phosphoric acid (H)
		Saccharine, sodium nitrate and nitrate (H)
		ALCOHOL

Synthetic: sodium bicarbonate, calcium chloride, calcium silicate, silicon dioxide, sodium benzoate, sodium citrate, acetic acid	Alanine (AN)
	ARTIFICIAL SWEETENERS (H)
	BEVERAGES
	  (Non-alcoholic) (H)
		ALCOHOLIC BEVERAGES
		ARTIFICIAL SWEETENERS
		  Cyclamates, saccharine, aspartame
		BACON, BACON BITS

AGAR	BHA, BHT	BLOOD
ALANINE (P)	BILE SALTS (AN)	CIDER (AL)
AMYLOSE	BIOTIN (AN)	COCAINE (H)
ANTIOXIDANTS	CAFFEINE (H)	CODEINE (H)
Vitamin C and E	CARBOHYDRATES (AN)	COLLAGEN (Hog)
ARTIFICIAL SWEETENERS	CHELATE (AN)	COLORING EXTRACTS
Sorbitol, mannitol	CHOLESTEROL (AN)	(Synthetics) (H)
ASCORBIC ACID (Vitamin C)	COFFEE (H)	DEAD ANIMALS
AVIDIN	COLORING EXTRACTS (H)	DES (female sex hormone)
BAKING SODA	COBALAMINE (AN)	ETHYLENE OXIDE
BENZOATE (Benzoic acid)	CYSTEINE (AN)	FERMENTED MALT (AL)
BRAN	CYSTINE (AN)	GELATIN (Hog)
BUTYRIC ACID	DIGLYCERIDES (AN)	HAM (Hog)
	DIURETICS (H)	

AL = Alcohol   AN = Animal origin   H = Health reasons   P = Plant origin

(Continued) A PARTIAL LIST OF CLASSIFIED INGREDIENTS AND ADDITIVES

LAWFUL (HALAL)	SUSPECTED (MASH-BOOH)	UNLAWFUL (HARAM)
CARBOHYDRATES (P)	EDTA (H)	INSULIN (Porcine)
CALCIFEROL (Vitamin D_3)	EMULSIFIERS (AN)	LARD (Hog)
CAROTENOID	ENZYMES (AN)	MEATS - Carnivorous (AN)
CARRAGEENAN	FATTY ACIDS (AN)	PEPSIN (Hog)
CASEIN	FLAVORING EXTRACTS (H)	PORK
CELLULOSE	FOLIC ACID (AN)	SHORTENING (AN)
CHOCOLATE LIQUOR	GALLIC ACID (H)	VANILLA EXTRACT (AL)
CHOLINE	GELATINE (AN)	VANILLIN EXTRACT (AL)
CITRIC ACID	GLYCERIDE (AN)	VITAMIN CAPSULES
DEXTRIN; DEXTROSE	GLYCEROL (AN)	(A, E, K) (AN)
DIGLYCERIDES (P)	GLYCOGEN (AN)	WINE
EMULSIFIERS (P)	HISTAMINE	
ERGOSTEROL	HORMONES (AN)	
FARINA	INSULIN (AN)	
FATTY ACIDS (P)	INOSITOL (AN)	
FIBERS	KERATIN (AN)	
FICIN	LIMIT DEXTRIN (AN)	
FOLIC ACID (P)	LIPIDS (AN)	
FRUCTOSE	MONOGLYCERIDE (AN)	
GALACTOSE	NIACIN (AN)	
GELATINE (Seaweeds or beef-knox)		

AL = Alcohol   AN = Animal origin   H = Health reasons   P = Plant origin

(Continued) A PARTIAL LIST OF CLASSIFIED INGREDIENTS AND ADDITIVES

LAWFUL (HALAL)	SUSPECTED (MASH-BOOH)	UNLAWFUL (HARAM)

GLIADIN (Gluten)
GLUCOSE (Dextrose)
GLYCERIDE (P)
GUMS
HEMICELLULOSE
HYDROGENATED OILS
INOSITOL (P)
INULIN
IODINE
LACTIC ACID
LACTOSE
LANOLIN
LECITHIN
LIPIDS (P)
LYSINE
MALT
MALTOSE
MOLASSES
MONOGLYCERIDE (P)
MONOSACCHARIDE
	OLEIC ACID (AN)
	OXALIC ACID (H)
	PEPSIN (AN)
	PABA (AN)
	PHOSPHOLIPID (AN)
	PHOSPHORIC ACID (H)
	PHYTIC ACID (H)
	POLYSACCHARIDE
	  (Glycogen)
	POLYUNSATURATED FATTY
	  ACIDS (AN)
	RENNET (AN)
	RENNIN (AN)
	RIBOFLAVIN (AN)
	SHORTENINGS (AN)
	STIMULANTS (H)
	SWEETENER (H)
	TARTARIC ACID (AL) .
	TEA (H)
	THIAMIN (AN)	

AL = Alcohol   AN = Animal origin   H = Health reasons   P = Plant origin

(Continued) A PARTIAL LIST OF CLASSIFIED INGREDIENTS AND ADDITIVES

LAWFUL (HALAL)	SUSPECTED (MASH-BOOH)	UNLAWFUL (HARAM)

OLEIC ACID (P)
PASTEURIZATION
PANTOTHENIC ACID
PAPAIN
PARA AMINO BENZOIC
  ACID (PABA)
PECTIN (P)
POLYSACCHARIDE (P)
POLYUNSATURATED FATTY
  ACIDS (P)
PROPIONIC ACID
RENNET (Microbial) (P)
RENNIN (Microbial) (P)
RIBOFLAVIN (P)
ROUGHAGE
SHORTENINGS (P)
SORBIC ACID
SORBITOL
STARCH
STIMULANTS
	TONIC (AL)
	TRYPSIN (AN)
	URIC ACID (AN)
	WATER (soft, carbonated) (H)
	WHEY (animal pepsin or rennin)
	YEAST (brewer's beer products)	

AL = Alcohol   AN = Animal origin   H = Health reasons   P = Plant origin

(Continued) A PARTIAL LIST OF CLASSIFIED INGREDIENTS AND ADDITIVES

LAWFUL (HALAL)	SUSPECTED (MASH-BOOH)	UNLAWFUL (HARAM)
SUCROSE SUET SWEETENERS (natural) TALLOW TANNIC ACID THIAMIN (P) TONIC (no alcohol) TAPIOCA TRYPSIN (no pork) VANILLA VANILLIC ACID VANILLIN VINEGAR VITAMIN TABLETS (A, D, E, C) ZEIN		

AL = Alcohol   AN = Animal origin   H = Health reasons   P = Plant origin

E. Halal Milk

A group of concerned individuals got involved into the idea that "All Milk is not Halal". They tried to educate the Muslims about milk being <u>not</u> Halal. Their assumption is that "some dairies use BST (Bovine Somatotropine Hormone) injections as well as the use of vitamin A and D". Therefore, they have waged a war against those who were using milk and its dairy products. They made arrangement with one dairy company <u>not</u> to add vitamin A and D.

Many Muslims in southern California as well as in Chicago were disturbed as to the news brought to their attention. One individual from southern California made arrangement with another individual from Chicago who has his own personal private organization. They produced fliers trying to inform the Muslims that the Milk that they are drinking is <u>not</u> Halal.

We tried to investigate with those individuals through the author of this book as well as through the Islamic Food and Nutrition Couoncil of America (IFANCA) as to the validity of their claims. From their own fliers they contradict themselves. The following is a partial list of questions that were raised to them. They did not answer anyone of them as yet.

1. In Islam everything is Halal unless it is specified as Haram.
2. No one can say for the Halal is Haram because he suspects something.

3. There should be proof for any claim that is made.
4. We requested them to supply us with the letters that they wrote to the milk industries, as well as the answers from those companies so that we will be able to verify the claimed statements. We have been waiting for an answer for about a year now.
5. We requested them to give us the list of the names of milk industries in the U.S.A. or at least in California and Illinois, so that correspondence will be established between us and them. At the same time, we want to help them to be professional and to be fact finders. They were unable to submit the list as requested.
6. The flier produced by those two individuals states that the source of Vitamin D_3 whole milk or the low fat milk is sheep lanolin. It is natural. At the same time, they claim it is un-natural, unclean and Haram. Such type of a statement cannot come from any respected student of science, research, technology, or food scientist.
7. In the same flier, they claim that Vitamin A comes from palm oil, calcium carbonate and palmitic acid. They claim it is Haram and unclean. Such a sentence does not come from any sound mind of any student of knowledge.
8. They stated that the sources of polysorbate 80 and glycerol-mono-oleate could be pork, beef, or plant. They are chemical

emulsifiers. Therefore, they are Haram and unclean. We don't understand how someone comes to a final conclusion and gives Fatwa of Haram or Halal on something that he himself does not know about. The question that we raised to those individuals was to ask the dairy companies about the sources of these emulsifiers before they come to conclusions. Unfortunately, up till now, they did not bring the information to the Muslim consumers.

Therefore, fliers of this nature do not mean anything to any student of knowledge. These fliers reflect immaturity on behalf of those who bring confusions to the Muslim consumers, when they themselves are not convinced as yet to the source(s) of these chemicals. Islam demands honesty, sincerity, and truthfulness of the information released to the consumers. Islamic teachings demand: (Al-Baiyna 'Ala Man Idda- 'aa).... Proof is to be given by those who claim anything. Also, Islam demands that we Muslims should seek knowledge from those who are wise, knowledgeable and honest.

Allah is the Greatest!

VITAMIN A & D PROCESS ADDED TO MILK

SOME DAIRIES USE BST HORMONE INJECTIONS

BST
- Unsure of cows food
- Cows forced to give much more milk than normal output
- Causes increased pus and bacteria in milk
- Causes sickness to cows and maybe to you and your family
- Unclean milk

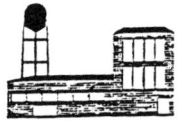

- Vitamin A & D Fortification Process added to milk
- Some ingredients unclean
- when pork is used - HARAM!

WHOLE MILK-VITAMIN D3 PROCESS ADDED TO YOUR MILK

INGREDIENTS	DERIVED FROM	DESCRIPTION
Vitamin D3	Sheep Lanolin	Natural
Water	Water	
Polysorbate 80	Pork, Beef, or Plant	Chemical emulsifiers
Proplyene glycol	Petroleum	Haram & unclean

LOWFAT & NONFAT - VITAMIN A&D PROCESS ADDED TO YOUR MILK

INGREDIENTS	DERIVED FROM	DESCRIPTION
Vitamin D3	Sheep Lanolin	Natural
Corn Oil	Corn	
Polysorbate 80	Pork, Beef, or Plant	Chemical emulsifiers
Glycerol - mono-oleate	Pork, Beef or Plant	Haram & unclean
Vitamin A palmitate	Palm oil, calcium carbonate and palmitic acid	

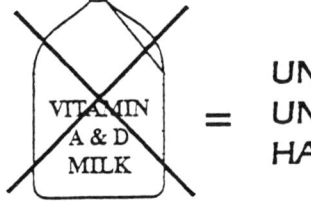

= UNNATURAL UNCLEAN HARAM

HALAL MILK PROCESS

NO INJECTION

- Consume natural food afalfa, oats, grain, hay no chemical additives
- Cows produce natural levels of milk output per day
- Clean milk

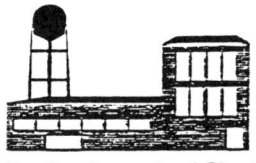

Muslim Supervised Plant

NOTHING ADDED TO MILK!

- Homogenized
- Pasteurized

Drink Halal Milk
Be Safe, Be Sure
Natural and Fresh
From Start to Finish
Clean and Pure

Available in
whole, lowfat, or non fat

HALAL MILK, 100% PURE

- No chemical vitamins (A&D3) or any additives
- Cows free of BST hormone injections
- No pork or animal by product used
- Certified Halal "H" by the Muslim Consumer Group
- Processed and distributed in the Halal manner under Strict Muslim Supervision to ensure Quality and Purity.
- Certified 100% Pure

F.   "Mad Cow"

The story of the 'Mad Cow' is a very interesting story to be mentioned here. It is reported in the L.A. Times, Saturday May 4, 1996 the following:

LOS ANGELES TIMES

'Mad Cow' Ban Strikes at Heart of British Identity

■ **Europe:** Beef, which has distinguished the nation from the Continent, now divides it from EU partners.

'I am a great eater of beef, and I believe that does harm to my wit.'
—**William Shakespeare**
"**Twelfth Night,**" **Act I, Scene 3**

By WILLIAM D. MONTALBANO
TIMES STAFF WRITER

LONDON—For centuries, proud Englishmen have willingly risked their wit for a hearty round of beef. Today, their heirs angrily recoil from international assault on a dish that is a cornerstone here of the national psyche.

"Since the 15th century, beef has been a symbol emphasizing the wealth of ordinary English people and of their robust, prosperous, common-sense culture and democracy," said David R. Starkey, a historian at the London School of Economics.

Furor zigzags across Europe six weeks after British beef was identified as the suspected source of an incurable human brain disease.

Bovine spongiform encephalopathy is the "mad cow" disease that may have leaped the species barrier in the past decade to infect almost a dozen people in Britain with a new strain of killer Creutzfeldt-Jakob disease.

But now it is the people here who are mad. English dander is up.

The international ban against the export of British beef, reaffirmed by the European Union at talks in Luxembourg this week, has

Please see BEEF, A12

No matter what politicians and farmers say the truth of the matter is as follows:

1. Cattles are herbivorous animals. Beef and cows are to be fed only from the plant kingdom.
2. Farmers have given steers female sex hormones such as Diethylstilbesterol to increase its size within a short period. It is a steroid hormone and it is a female sex hormone.
3. Cows have been given estrogen hormone to increase the size of its milk bladder and accordingly to increase its milk secretion.
4. Cattles were fed dead animals. The feed industry takes dead animals and dries them. Then they grind them and mix them with dry plants and prepare food for animals.
5. Cattles are given even pork (dead animals) as food. They are given also blood in a dry form mixed with other materials.
6. The dead animals might be sick. The diseases were tansformed from the sick- dead- animals to the living animals.
7. The "Mad Cows" ended up with a disease called Bovine Spongiform Encephalopathy (BSE) which transformed to human beings. Ironically, BSE has been twisted as: "Blame Somebody Else".

In the magazine of Food Technology, May 1996 page 312 (see caption on the next page), Susan Brewer and Jan Novakofski under the title of Mad Cow Disease, say the following:

FOOD TECHNOLOGY BACK PAGE

SUSAN BREWER and JAN NOVAKOFSKI

Mad Cow Disease

Bovine Spongiform Encephalopathy, commonly referred to as "mad cow disease", is a fatal brain disease of cattle. Its prevention or eradication is of primary importance to safeguard herds and the future supply of dairy and bovine meat products for human and pet foods.

A transmissible spongiform encephalopathy of cattle was first diagnosed in Great Britain in 1986. BSE is one of a group of degenerative diseases which occur in several species. Britain is th only country with a high incidence of the disease; more than 155,000 cases have been identified. The disease has been confirmed in Ireland, France, Portugal, and Switzerland, and in cattle exported from England to Oman, the Falkland Islands, Germany, Denmark, Canada, and Italy. No case of BSE has been confirmed in the United States.

> Cattle affected by BSE experience progressive degeneration of the nervous system and display changes in temperament (nervousness or aggression); abnormal posture; incoordination and difficulty in rising; decreased milk production; or loss of body weight despite continued appetite.

The primary causes of the BSE as being stated by these two authors would be:

> Epidemiological evidence indicates that the primary cause of BSE in Britain was likely to have been the use of commercial cattle feed containing meat and bone meal derived from sheep (and possibly cattle) presumed to have been infected.

Some other related diseases may be correlated with this deadly disease. According to these authors other disease includes the following:

> Scrapie, which affects sheep and goats; mink encephalopathy; feline spongiform encephalophathy; chronic wasting disease of mule deer and elk; and kuru, Creutzfeldt-Jakob disease (CJD), and Gerstmann-Straussier syndrome (GSS), three rare diseases in humans.

What needs to be done accordingly is:

> The banning of ruminant material from animal

feed stuffs in Britain has led to a dramatic decline in new cases. This may be seen as confirming the feedstuff hypothesis. It lends support to the view that if control measures are strictly adhered to, the disease will not become a problem in the U.S.

Allah (swt) specified for us in the Qur'an what to eat and what to drink. Our beloved Prophet (pbuh) explained to us the details of this injunction. Human beings are to eat the herbevorous animals. Their feed should be from the plant kingdom. No hormones are to be given to them. If they eat animal meat, they should be isolated (40) days before being slaughtered. Then at the time of slaughtering, the butcher is to mention the name of Allah (swt).

Any preservative added to the meat later should not be toxic or to cause any sickness. Therefore, all these factors are conditions for th meat to be called Halal.

The following Headlines are examples of some of the articles that were printed in the Los Angeles Times, May 1996.

LOS ANGELES TIMES

BEEF: Thousands of Cows to Be Destroyed

Continued from A12

Agence France-Presse
British Agriculture Minister Douglas Hogg is fighting the beef ban.

Los Angeles Times

SATURDAY, MAY 4, 1996

Program to Destroy Cattle Gets Underway

■ **Health:** Culling of possibly diseased animals is expected to reach 3,000 a day.

By WILLIAM D. MONTALBANO
TIMES STAFF WRITER

Stuart Shaw feeds his cattle herd on his farm in central England.

LONDON—The destruction of cattle considered most at risk from "mad cow disease" got off to a halting start Friday with more bureaucratic tangles than drama.

About 100 cows older than 30 months were slaughtered in Scotland, stained with an indelible yellow dye and then sent to be rendered, keeping them out of the food chain.

Thousands more animals will be destroyed and their remains incinerated as the program gathers speed next week.

The government-ordered cull is aimed at restoring consumer confidence in British beef and encouraging the European Union to lift an international export ban imposed in March after reports of a possible but unproven link between bovine spongiform encephalopathy, or BSE, and an incurable human brain disorder, Creutzfeldt-Jakob disease.

Agriculture Minister Douglas Hogg had announced that a 3,000-head-a-day cull would begin earlier this week, but the establishment of about 100 collection and killing centers and other arrangements delayed the start of a process that will likely last years.

Under the program, according to representatives of the National Farmers Union, farmers will decide—as they do now—when to send their cattle to market. But older animals will be destroyed and rendered to avoid any chance of human consumption.

With the European Union paying 70% of the cull costs, farmers have been told to expect about $1.50 per pound live weight for their animals.

The cull will eliminate mostly dairy cattle, which can be productive for many years and which have been hardest hit by BSE.

Earliest targets, though, will be older beef cattle.

Since the crisis began six weeks ago, farmers have been feeding those herds without any prospect of selling them for meat.

In all, as many as 750,000 of the animals slaughtered in Britain in the coming year will be destroyed without any use of meat or byproducts.

Britain claims that the export ban is disproportionate and unjust.

The $6-billion-a-year industry is still reeling from the crisis, but British consumers are already returning to beef. Consumption has rebounded to about 85% of its pre-crisis level, according to the Meat and Livestock Commission, and British beef is beginning to reappear at supermarkets and restaurants.

BSE has killed about 160,000 British cows in the past decade.

It is believed to have been introduced to British herds in high-protein feeds containing the ground remains of infected sheep.

That practice is now banned. Older animals are at the greatest risk from BSE because the disease has a long incubation period.

In addition to a cull supported by farmers, the British government is also proposing the enforced slaughter of 42,000 animals in herds where BSE has been most prevalent. European agriculture officials, though, told Hogg in Luxembourg this week that they want a more sweeping cull before deciding whether to relax the ban.

G. Why is Halal Supervision Necessary?

Many food industries these days are interested to certify their food products. Some of the major problems they face are: Zabiha (Halal) meat, ingredients, preservatives, the gelatineous covering of the capsules for vitamins, medicinal and pharmaceutical products. Since Muslims in their home-lands are importing these products from non-Muslim countries, it became imperative to supervise the industries and to certify their products.

In th following section, the Islamic Food and Nutrition Council of America (IFANCA) has written a statement about this subject. It is felt that it is a good idea to include it here:

Recent advances in food science and technology have made it very imperative that foods manufactured for Muslims should be closely monitored so that they meet the requirements as stipulated in the Islamic Laws.

The Muslim consumer worldwide is becoming more aware and conscious of the need for halal foods and this has put tremendous pressure on manufacturers and producers to comply with these requirements.

Universally, many different Muslim countries still import substantial amounts of foodstuffs and meat from Western countries. With the growing trend towards authentic halal foods, the importing countries make it a requisite that foods imported carry halal certification issued by Islamic organizations approved by the importing countries.

Constant information needs to be carried out to make more manufacturers comply with the Islamic requirements in totality. Practice of slaughtering animals for Muslim consumption needs to be strictly supervised, because many large companies mislabel commercial meat as halal or slaughtered according to Islamic Law.

Needless to say, proper supervision will help weed out the unscrupulous manufacturer / producer who is in for a quick profit. The point that has to be emphatically made is that if the manufacturer wants to continue selling genuine halal food, he has to be sensitive to the aspirations of the Muslim Ummah and establish close rapport with the various Islamic Organizations. The cost of halal supervision is not very expensive and certainly affordable.

In reality, the producers and exporters are going to realize more profits due to an increase in their sales.

Most importantly, producing the meat products under the supervision of reputable halal certifying organization will certainly eliminate the type of problems we see in the products imported to Muslim countries; such as pork mixed into beef, gelatin in candies, etc.

H. Pork Slaughtered According to Islamic Law

A very shocking news was reported in the Arabic newspaper of Al-Muslimoon, published in Riyadh, Saudi Arabia. In the issue of (486) 10th year, Friday 16 Zul Hijjah 1414, corresponding May 27, 1994. The title of the news article is:

Pork Slaughtered According to Islamic Law!!

Due to the importance of this subject, we are including the translation of that article in English, keeping the caption of the article as seen in that newspapaer of Al-Muslimoon.

Therefore, certification and regular supervision by qualified Muslims are essential to safeguard any wrong-doing anywhere in the world.

<u>Abu Dhabi.</u> According to local sources, several foreign companies are exporting meat labelled beef to Muslim countries, which in reality contains pork, stating that it has been slaughtered according to the Islamic Law.

By doing so, they are trying to break the prohibitions imposed by Islam on this kind of meat and are trying to make the Muslims become used to it without their knowledge or awareness.

Sources at the General Secretariat of the Municipalities of the United Arab Emirates said "This year they banned seven types of canned meat and dessert products due to pork meat and its by-products in their ingredient statements. Many of the items they removed from the markets are very popular among Muslim consumers in Arab and Islamic markets, and these were basic meals in the schools due to ease of preparation.

It is not clear as to when these companies might have started mixing certain quantities of pork and lard into their products, according to the sources who related this to Al-Muslimoon. According to the same sources the Municipalities have recently started checking very strictly for detection in such canned meat products.

Same sources said that some of the Municipalities have started a very strict survey of canned meat after it was discovered accidentally that a small shipment of luncheon meat made by a well-known Dutch company "Zwan" had contradictory label statements on the cans.

On one side of the can, under the ingredients, the company put in the English language "contains pork", on the other side of the can it read in Arabic, "Slaughtered according to Islamic Law".

One of the consumers noticed this discrepency in the city of Ajman and brought it to the municipality's attention.

A food inspector at Sharjah's municipality examined several samples from many products of the kind mentioned above, and found them to contain pork. As a result, the company representatives were summoned. The company representatives concurred that the test results were indeed correct and confessed that there was a small amount of pork and lard in those products. The representatives also said that the company produces beef and pork products on the same line. The said products were made on the equipment used for pork, without thorough and proper cleaning before making beef products for export to the Muslim countries.

The company announced to the press that it is willing to withdraw the implicated products from the market in an effort to create counter pressure on the media and the Emirates. A company official in the capital of Holland declared that the company will lose 2.5 million dollars if the UAE government decided that the contaminated shipments must be destroyed. He also said that the company wishes to send those products to some other markets which do not have such restrictions for pork.

On the other hand, General Secretariat of UAE municipalities had declared that they will ban the shipments of <u>Zavan products</u> and order the removal of the same from the market.

It will request the Municipality of Sharjah to have the product destroyed and ban the import of any further shipments from <u>Zavan</u> Company.

A reliable source from the General Secretariat mentioned that Sharjah municipality has already started testing, on its own, different canned meat samples, produced by several companies. There are a myriad of commonly used products in the local market. It has been discovered by Sharjah Municipality that the <u>Emory</u> brand luncheon meat products, produced in Holland and <u>Heinz</u> and <u>Castlon</u> brands have pork in the ingredient statements. The findings had been submitted to the Secretariat of the Municipalities, which decided to ban the products of the companies mentioned above and prohibit them to carry their products in all markets there.

It was also discovered by the Municipalities during the tests that the candies for children where gelatin was used, was another target area by the food producing companies, especially those companies who were aware of the restrictions. They intentionally and maliciously incorporated pork and pork by-products into good food to make their use widespread in Islamic countries.

The General Secretariat of the Municipalities recently discovered that gelatin - containing desserts of American name brand Swift & Philippine's brand Rica, and German brand Coast contain a high percentage of pork by-products.

A statement issued by the General Secretariat assured that every necessary legal action will be taken against the above companies and import and entry of their products will be banned.

I. Vitamins

Many consumers are propounded with too many information about foods, liquids, vitamins, minerals, food supplements, food enrichments, food preservatives, catalysts, enzymes, microbial fermentation, weight control using different methods of dieting, and so on and so forth.

In this section, the author wishes to reflect few ideas about food supplementation. To be more specific: Milk enrichment with vitamin A & D will be discussed. Both of these vitamins are among the series of vitamins which are considered to be Fat-Soluble vitamins. They are vitamin A, D, E, and K. The Water-Soluble vitamins are the B - Complex vitamins and vitamin C. The B - Complex vitamin is categorized as B_1, B_2, Niacin, B_6, B_{12}, Follic Acid, Pantothenic Acid, Biotin, and Vitamin C. Please see the Table of these vitamins as well as their material sources and their role in the body.

As far as vitamin A is concerned, its natural source is Fish Liver Oil. Please see Merk Index on pp. 1434 and the book of Family Guide to Natural Medicine on pps. 278 & 279. As far as vitamin D_3 is concerned, its natural source also comes from Fish Liver Oil. Please see Merk Index, page 1436.

From an industrial and commercial point of view, any corporation is to choose the most available in the local market as well as the most inexpensive; otherwise, it will not survive anywhere in the world. When vitamin A and D are available in fish liver oil, no one with sound mind is going to get those vitamins from beef, lamb, or pork. The most available and the most inexpensive is fish liver oil.

For research purposes, scientists try to compare and contrast all possible sources to find out the potency of each element, as well as for each molecule or compound. Scientists by nature have to try all possible means even if the materials are the most expensive; otherwise, they are not scientists.

In every industry of food, medicine, pharmacy, and other corporations, they have a Department called Research and Development (R&D). These scientists in such departments spend days, months, and years doing their own research to find out the most suitable, the most inexpensive, and the most available. As such they find the best. It is only then that they will develop it for use at the most profitable basis to their own company. Even before bringing it to public, they have to take the approval of the Food and Drug Agency (FDA) of USA; and sometimes the approval of US Department of Agriculture (USDA).

There are some individuals who are bookish, while others are not scientists. There is a group of individuals who might be scientists but in other fields of speciality.

One might find a group of business people who are after money. They recruite someone with an academic title to write for them to suite their needs. The final result is confusion and distortion of information.

Our recommendation to the consumer is not to rush and believe everything you hear or read. Take time! Ask the `Alims, and ask more than one scientist. Go to Muslim scientists who love Allah (swt) and His Messenger (pbuh). Don't take it for grant it from any business man. Most of the business people are after profits. We don't blame them and we don't condemn anyone. However, we are for the consumers, and we are to protect the rights of these innocent buyers so that they will not be confused by the advertisments of the business people.

We pray to Allah (swt) to guide all of us to the right path, and to grant us wisdom so that we write the truth, and we speak only the truth. Ameen!

USE: For blood volume determinations.

9818. Vitamin A. Retinol; 3,7-dimethyl-9-(2,6,6-trimethyl-1-cyclohexen-1-yl)-2,4,6,8-nonatetraen-1-ol; anti-infective vitamin; lard-factor; antixerophthalmic vitamin; axerophthol; biosterol; oleovitamin A; ophthalamin (obsolete); vitamin A_1; vitamin A alcohol; Acon; Afaxin; Agiolan; Alphalin; Anatola; Aoral; Apexol; Apostavit; Atav; Avibon; Avita; Avitol; Axerol; "Dohyfral" A; Epiteliol; Nio-A-Let; Prepalin; Testavol; Vaflol; Vi-Alpha; Vitpex; Vogan; Vogan-Neu. $C_{20}H_{30}O$; mol wt 286.44. C 83.86%, H 10.56%, O 5.59%. Occurs in the animal organism (not in plants); carotenoids are converted into vitamin A by the liver. Extracted from fish liver oils where it occurs mostly in esterified form. Structure: Karrer et al., Helv. Chim. Acta **14**, 1036, 1431; Karrer, Morf, ibid. **16**, 625 (1933); Heilbron et al., Biochem. J. **26**, 1178, 1194 (1932). Stereochemistry: see L. Zechmeister, Chem. Rev. **34**, 267 (1944). Identity of lard-factor and vitamin A: Ames, Harris, Science **120**, 391 (1954). Total synthesis of vitamin A from β-ionone and a propargyl halide: Eiter, Truscheit, U.S. pat. 3,060,229 (1962 to Bayer); by conversion of vitamin A aldehyde: Wendler et al., J. Am. Chem. Soc. **72**, 234 (1950); Klein, Kapp, U.S. pat. 2,972,634 (1961 to Nopco); by reduction of retinal, q.v.: T. Mukaiyama, A. Ishida, Chem. Letters **1975**, 1201. Stereospecific synthesis of all (E)-form: P. S. Manchand et al., Helv. Chim. Acta **59**, 567 (1976); A. Fischli et al., ibid. 397; G. Cardillo et al., J. Chem. Soc., Perkin Trans. I **1979**, 1729. Comprehensive monograph of the chemistry, physics, physiology of vitamin A and its provitamins: W. H. Sebrell, R. S. Harris, The Vitamins. Vol. I (Academic Press, New York, 2nd ed., 1967) 570 pp. See also: Neovitamin A.

Yellow prisms from propylene oxide or petr ether. Solvated crystals from more polar solvents, such as methanol or ethyl formate. mp 62-64°. Distills at 120-125° at 5 × 10^{-3} mm pressure. n_D^{25} 1.6410 (calculated from refractive indexes of 20-70% solns in mineral oil). uv max: 324-325 nm ($E_{1cm}^{1\%}$ 1835); Baxter, Robeson, J. Am. Chem. Soc. **64**, 2407 (1942). Practically insol in water or glycerol; sol in abs alcohol, methanol, chloroform, ether, fats and oils. Ultraviolet light inactivates vitamin A and its solns which exhibit a characteristic green fluorescence. The free alcohol is sensitive to air-oxidation, but oil solns of it are quite stable. Esters of vitamin A are more stable to oxidation.
Acetate. $C_{22}H_{32}O_2$, pale yellow prismatic crystals from methanol. mp 57-58°. uv max (ethanol): 326 nm ($E_{1cm}^{1\%}$ 1550). Biopotency 2.904 × 10^6 I.U./g.
Palmitate. $C_{36}H_{60}O_2$, Arovit, is the ester preponderant in fish liver oils. Amorphous or cryst. mp 28-29°. uv max: 325-328 nm ($E_{1cm}^{1\%}$ 975). Biopotency 1.817 × 10^6 I.U./g.
Note: The U.S.P. unit of vitamin A is equal to 0.30 microgram of vitamin A equivalent to 0.344 microgram of vitamin A acetate. Observed biopotency 3.33 × 10^6 I.U./g.
THERAP CAT: Antixerophthalmic vitamin.
THERAP CAT (VET): Nutritional factor.

9819. Vitamin A_2. 3,4-Didehydroretinol; retinol$_2$; dehydroretinol. $C_{20}H_{28}O$; mol wt 284.42. C 84.45%, H 9.92%, O 5.63%. Combines with opsin to form the visual pigment, porphyropsin. q.v., in fresh-water fish. A mixture of stereoisomers. Isoln from pike liver oils: Shantz, Science **108**, 417 (1948). See also Shantz, Brinkman, J. Biol. Chem. **183**, 467 (1950); Farrar et al., J. Chem. Soc. **1952**, 503. Synthesis and characteristics of stereoisomers: Schwieter, Chimia **14**, 362 (1960); Helv. Chim. Acta **45**, 517, 528, 541, 548 (1962). Review: The Vitamins. vol. 1, W. H. Sebrell, R. S. Harris, Eds. (Academic Press, New York, 2nd ed., 1967) passim.

9830. Vitamin D$_3$. *9,10-Secocholesta-5,7,10(19)-trien-3-ol;* activated 7-dehydrocholesterol; oleovitamin D$_3$; cholecalciferol; colecalciferol; CC; Duphafral D$_3$ 1000; Delsterol; Deparal; Ebivit; Micro-Dee; Neo Dohyfral D$_3$; Provitina; Ricketon; Trivitan; D$_3$-Vicotrat; Vi-De-3-hydrosol; Vigantol; Vigorsan. C$_{27}$H$_{44}$O; mol wt 384.62. C 84.31%, H 11.53%, O 4.16%. The vitamin that mediates intestinal calcium absorption, bone calcium metabolism and probably, muscle activity. It usually acts as a hormone precursor as it requires two stages of metabolism, first to 25-hydroxycholecalciferol, *q.v.*, and then to 1α,25-dihydroxycholecalciferol, *q.v.*, before reaching actual hormonal form. Occurs in and is isolated from fish liver oils. Methods of sepn include chromatography, molecular distillation, esterification and fractionation of the esters. Prepd by irradiation of its provitamin 7-dehydrocholesterol, *q.v.*: Windaus *et al., Z. Physiol. Chem.* **241**, 100 (1936); Windaus *et al., Ann.* **533**, 118 (1938); Akhtar, Gibbons, *Tetrahedron Letters* **1965**, 509. Direct total synthesis: B. Lythgoe *et al., Tetrahedron Letters* **1977**, 3685. Laser photochemical production: V. Malatesta *et al., J. Am. Chem. Soc.* **103**, 6781 (1981). General review: Inhoffen, *Angew. Chem.* **72**, 875-881 (1960). Review of metabolism: Haussler, Rasmussen, *J. Biol. Chem.* **247**, 2328-2335 (1972); *Nature* **245**, 180-182 (1973).

Fine needles from dilute acetone, mp 84-85°. $[\alpha]_D^{20}$ +84.8° (c = 1.6 in acetone); $[\alpha]_D^{20}$ +51.9° (c = 1.6 in chloroform). uv max (alcohol or hexane): 264.5 nm. (E$_{1cm}^{1\%}$ 450-490): Huber *et al., J. Am. Chem. Soc.* **67**, 609 (1945). Not precipitated by digitonin (diff from 7-dehydrocholesterol). Practically insol in water; sol in the usual organic solvents; slightly sol in vegetable oils. Oxidized and inactivated by moist air within a few days. Deterioration of pure cryst vitamin D$_3$ is negligible after storage of 1 year in amber evacuated ampuls at refrigerator temps; vitamin D$_2$ may be kept for 9 months under the same conditions. Additional stability information: Huber, Barlow, *J. Biol. Chem.* **149**, 125 (1942). Generally vitamin D$_3$ is considered more stable than vitamin D$_2$.

Note: Vitamin D$_3$ is approx as effective as vitamin D$_2$ in the human and in the rat. It is also fully active in chicks. Vitamin D$_2$ is only 1-2 percent as potent for the chick as vitamin D$_3$. Because of this difference it is important that poultry feeds are supplemented with vitamin D$_3$ rather than D$_2$. One unit (U.S.P. or international) is defined as the activity of 0.025 γ of vitamin D$_3$ contained in the U.S.P. vitamin D reference standard.

THERAP CAT: Antirachitic vitamin.

	Vitamin	Main Role	Good Food Sources
Fat Soluble	**A** *(retinol)*	Needed for maintenance of skin, mucous membranes, bones, teeth, and hair; vision; and reproduction.	Retinol sources: fish liver oils, egg yolks, butter, cream. Beta-carotene sources: leafy green and yellow vegetables.
	D *(calciferol)*	Helps body absorb calcium and phosphorous; needed for bone growth and maintenance.	Vitamin-D fortified milk and milk products, margarine, egg yolks, fish liver oils, liver.
	E *(tocopherol)*	Helps form red blood cells; prevents oxidation damage.	Vegetable oils, nuts, seeds, green leafy vegetables, whole grains.
	K	Needed for blood clotting.	Green leafy vegetables, vegetable oils, egg yolks, liver.
Water Soluble	B_1 *(thiamin)*	Needed for nervous system function; helps release energy from carbohydrates.	Whole grains, enriched breads and cereals, seeds, nuts, legumes, dried yeast, potatoes, pork, kidney, liver.
	B_2 *(riboflavin)*	Helps release energy from foods.	Green leafy vegetables, enriched breads and cereals, fish, poultry, milk and milk products, liver, meat.
	Niacin	Needed for nervous and digestive system functions; helps release energy from foods.	Enriched bread and cereals, poultry, fish, legumes, liver, meat.

Main Role	Good Food Sources	Water Soluble
Needed for metabolism; helps form red blood cells.	Dried yeast, whole grains, fish, legumes, bananas, nuts, potatoes.	B_6 (pyridoxine)
Helps form red blood cells; contributes to neural function.	Liver, meats, seafood, eggs, milk and milk products.	B_{12} (cobalamin)
Helps form red blood cells and genetic material.	Leafy green vegetables, fruit, whole grains, legumes.	Folic acid
Helps metabolize nutrients.	Whole grains, legumes, green leafy vegetables, milk, egg yolks, liver, kidney.	Pantothenic acid
Involved in metabolism of fatty acids; helps release energy from carbohydrates and amino acids.	Cauliflower, liver, egg yolk, legumes, nuts.	Biotin
Promotes formation, growth, and maintenance of bones and teeth; repair of tissues; resistance to infection.	Citrus fruits, tomatoes, potatoes, cabbage, green peppers.	C (ascorbic acid)

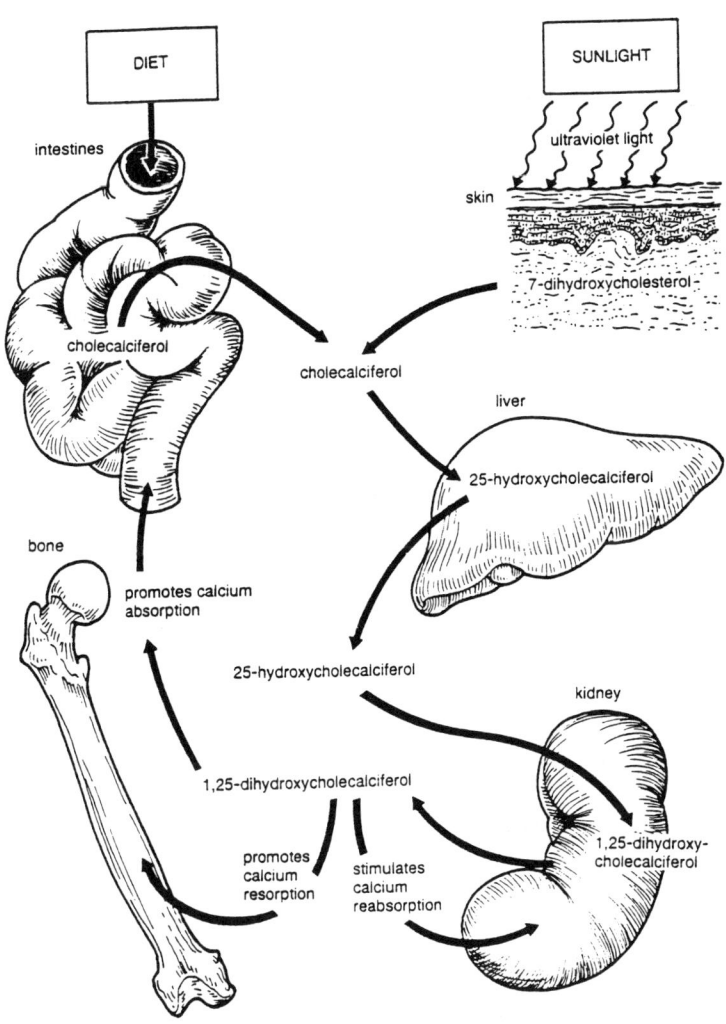

Figure 60.1 Vitamin D metabolism

J. USDA & Muslim Foods

Some communications took place between the United State Department of Agriculture (USDA), Food and Consumer Service, Mid-Atlantic Region and the author of this book. Official personnel in USDA were concerned about meals and menus for Muslim children and families as well. They made a survey using different Muslim books and by communicating with different Muslim scholars. They came with a piece of document which is very helpful to Muslims and non-Muslims as well. Such a document is also helpful to public school systems in preparing menus that are devoid of pork and its bi-products. Moreover, the document spelled out the ideas of Halal (Zabiha), Haram, Makrooh, and Mashbooh as well. The practice of fasting is also included. A partial list of Halal, Haram ingredients is also included.

An official document such as this, coming from USDA is very important to all in the long run. Because of its significance, part of it is included in this section.

**United States Department of Agriculture
Food and Consumer Service
Mid-Atlantic Region
Mercer Corporate Park
300 Corporate Boulevard
Robbinsville, N.J. 08691-1598**

Date: FEB 29 1996

Reply to Attention of:

Child Day Care Center Memo #11-96
Family Day Care Memo #14-96

Subject: Meal Pattern Guidance: Special Variations to Meet Ethnic and/or Religious Needs: Muslim Dietary Guidelines

To: Virginia Day Care Center Administrators
Virginia Family Day Home Sponsoring Organizations

We increasingly receive requests for information regarding Child and Adult Care Food Program (CACFP) meal pattern guidance to address ethnic and/or religious needs of children in day care.

Section 226.20 (I) of the CACFP regulations stipulates that USDA may approve variations in the food components of a meal where there is evidence that such variations are nutritionally sound where there is evidence that such variations are nutritionally sound and are necessary to meet ethnic, religious, economic, or physical needs. For example, FCS Instruction 783-13 addresses variations in meal requirements for Jewish schools and institutions, and FCS Instruction 783-14 addresses variations in meal requirements for Seventh-Day Adventist schools and institutions.

It is important to note that the program regulations do not require that variations be made for religious or ethnic reasons, however, many of you have expressed the desire to do so whenever it is practical and reasonable.

This guidance has been written for those centers or homes with a number of Muslim families and who wish to provide meals for those Muslim children who may have some dietary restrictions.

We also have prepared a more detailed guidance packet if you are interested in exploring this topic in greater depth. It contains specific restrictions, background about the relation between diet and faith, and suggested further readings. We will be happy to provide this document to you upon request: please contact Doris Lewis of this office at (609) 259-5072.

This overview, however, should meet the needs of most persons interested in adjusting menus to meet the dietary needs of the majority of Muslim families in the United States.

It is most important of all to recognize that each child and the members of its family are unique individuals. Within any group there is a wide variety of values, practices and beliefs. There is as much diversity within any group as between groups. Persons of the Muslim faith come from many different countries; each with its own rich food culture. Certain restrictions may be extremely important to the families in your community while other practices will not be issues for your families at all.

Your best resource is the child's family for clarification of the meal pattern adjustments needed to respect their particular beliefs and dietary restrictions. With the cooperation of your families, you can develop a food service plan that meets all of your families needs and is practical for the people who prepare your meals.

It is the responsibility of the Muslim family to identify food restrictions for you. If you decide that you will adjust your menus to meet the dietary needs of the Muslim families in your community, we encourage you to use the attached general survey. Remind families that the survey only covers dietary prohibitions not individual food preferences or medical considerations for the child. CACFP policy regarding procedures for obtaining medical exemptions remains current. Please contact us if you need further guidance on medical exemptions.

The completion of this form by the involved families will give you an idea of the types of adjustments that your center will wish to consider. You can then make a decision whether such changes are realistic for your program based upon your general and food preparation facilities, staffing levels, finances or other circumstances. If you decide that your center does not have the ability or resources to make such changes, you can then discuss possible options and alternatives which are acceptable for the families.

Please note that the majority of foods are considered to be Halal or lawful foods. There are a few foods considered to be Haram or unlawful. The majority of unlawful foods actually are not eaten by most people in the United States and would not appear on a menu because these are foods that simply would not be eaten by children.

The following foods are among those prohibited by different Muslim families. These foods are pork and its bi-products, alcohol, meat of already dead animals, animals slaughtered in a name other than that of Allah (swt), products made with blood, intoxicating substances such as tobacco and caffeine based products such as coffee, tea, or sodas.*

Fish are considered lawful. However, there is a difference of opinion among respected authorities regarding consumption of shellfish. If you wish to serve shellfish on your menu, we urge you to consult your family advisors as to their particular beliefs. Usually, however, shellfish are not served in child nutrition programs due to their high cost, low acceptability and because of the potential for food intolerance of some children.

---

* For health reasons. [ED]

While some religious families must eat meat which is slaughtered following specific religious procedures, the majority do not require such accommodation. If, however, your families indicate that this is an issue for them on the survey, you will want to ask yourselves the following: Can you obtain this meat, is it within cost consideration? If you do not choose to or are unable to purchase this meat, what other choices can you offer families to meet the meat/meat alternate component of the meat pattern? Can your program realistically make this accommodation, the answer will vary.

Obviously, of food which is prepared for children, only the use of pork and pork bi-products would be issues which might be generally raised when you are preparing menus of meals to be served to children. Since other groups of children, often can not eat pork for religious reasons, programs where this is an issue have already developed menu accommodations or offer alternatives.

If you have any questions or comments about this information you may call our NET Coordinator Michele Bouchard. She may be reached at (609) 259-5053.

RICHARD MALLAM, Section Chief
Day Care and Summer Nutrition Programs

Attachment

CHECKLIST

Determine what are the religious beliefs of the families in your program ask the following:

> What, if any foods are you and your children prohibited from eating based upon your religious beliefs?

> If prohibited foods are on the menu, what other choices are acceptable to you?

> Are there any food preparation techniques which are prohibited based upon your religious beliefs?

> If your child has food restriction based upon religious beliefs will you be willing to serve in an advisory capacity in menu planning for our program?

Since we wish to accommodate the religious food based restrictions of our children to the best of our ability, please indicate your name, address and children names if you have indicated restrictions for your children. In this way, we are aware and can be responsive to your child's needs.

United States Department of Agriculture
Food and Consumer Service
Mid-Atlantic Region
Mercer Corporate Park
300 Corporate Boulevard
Robbinsville, N.J. 08691-1598

Meeting the Nutritional Needs of Various Groups of Children:

Islamic Dietary Laws and Practices:

I. Meeting the Nutritional Needs of Various Groups of Children: Islamic Dietary Laws and Practices:

It is most important of all to recognize that each child and the members of its family are unique individuals. Within any group there is a wide variety of values, practices and beliefs. There is as much diversity within any group as between groups. Persons of the Muslim faith come from many different countries; each with its own rich food culture. Common sense tells us that any guide can only be that, a guide. The information presented in this fact sheet serves as a reference point for planning meals which respect the tenets of a child's faith, provide healthful meals which meet meal pattern requirements, and which taste good to the child.

Since current literature indicates that some differences of interpretation of dietary laws exist among recognized and respected religious authorities, your best resource is the child's family for clarification of the meal pattern adjustments needed to respect their particular beliefs and dietary restrictions.

Meal planning for a child or group of children who follow Islamic dietary laws and practices need not be a difficult task. It involves an awareness of food restrictions and the religious philosophy upon which practices are based. Certain practices will be extremely important to the families in your community, other practices will not be issues for your families.

Information in this fact sheet has been abstracted from the

following publications. Both books are highly recommended for persons wishing to read further information:

Islamic Dietary Laws and Practices written by Mohammad Mazhar Hussaini, M.S. and Ahmad Hussein Sakr, Ph.D. 1984. Islamic Food and Nutrition Council of America: Chicago, Illinois. pp 165.

This book logically presents detailed information about Islamic dietary laws in terms understandable to the lay person. An excellent resource for those wishing to learn more information. This book also contains sample recipes and extensive resource lists.

A Muslim Guide to Food Ingredients written by Ahmad Hussein Sakr, Ph.D. 1993. Foundation for Islamic Knowledge: Lombard, Illinois. pp 195.

This book is a comprehensive research resource providing detailed information about the majority of ingredients in the various foods and food products available in the market. The guide describes the composition of foods, specifies the plant or animal origin of the food and provides processing information where relevant. Foods are classified in the Halal, Makrooh, Mashbooh or Haram categories. The text provides clear explanations regarding the reasons for classification. Classifications are based upon religious, scientific and health perspectives. An outstanding tool for those preparing meals which consider Islamic dietary laws.

Melting Pot: An Annotated Bibliography and Guide to Food and Nutrition Information for Ethnic Groups in America. Edited By Jacqueline Newman. Second Edition. 1993. Garland Publishing: New York, New York. pp 240.

Ms. Newman's book represents a brief nutritional overview of each of the Muslim countries. She provides bibliographies of specific research for each geographical area. Ms. Newman also discusses foods which might be familiar to families in each culture. The book includes a bibliography of recommended cookbooks.

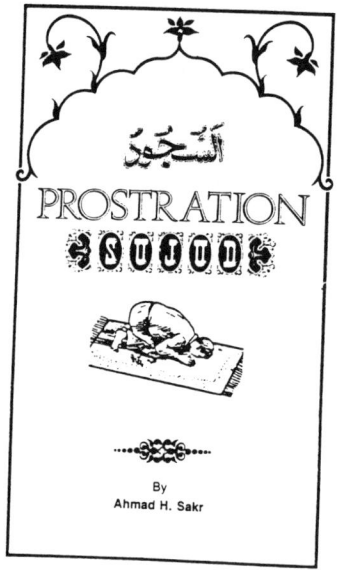

K.   Diet of Muslim Inmates

In June 1995, there was a dispute between the inmates in the state of Connecticut against the state officials. The Muslim inmates were given food where the menus contain pork and/or pork bi-products. The inmates requested the officials to have Muslim foods. It seems the state representatives found certain excuses not to supply them with Halal foods. Accordingly, the inmates took their case to the court.

The state of Connecticut recruited experts in the field of nutrition, food services, medical doctor, and Christian reverents and some Imams who are employed by the state as chaplains.

The inmates requested the local Islamic Center to support their demands. The name of the author of this book was recommended. The inmates were thrilled. The author was drafted to defend the demands of the Muslim inmates. The qualification of the author was scruitinized. The state of Connecticut finally agreed. Instead of inviting the author to go to the court to testify, the District Attourney of the state made a deposition for two and a half hours, trying to verify the information. He realized that the author should not come over to the court. Finally, he had agreed to allow the Muslim inmates to receive Halal (Muslim) foods. The following is the summary of the statements presented by the lawyer of the inmates:

Factual Allegations

I.   Dietary Requirements:

1. Plaintiffs are adherents of the Islamic religion and, as such, are bound by the sacred laws and traditions of Islam. Orthodox Muslims believe the law, as revealed in the Qur'an, to be the command of Allah (swt), the word of God, and provides the guidelines by which they conduct their lives. All actions which conform to the laws of Islam are considered to be Halal, or lawful. Those actions in contradiction to the teachings of the Qur'an are considered Haram, or unlawful.

2. Islamic law requires that meat be slaughtered and prepared in ritual fashion. As faithful Muslim adherents, each plaintiff is required by Islamic law to eat only meat prepared in accordance with religious law. Such meat is known as "Halal".

3. In accordance with the prescribed teachings of the Qur'an, in order for an animal to be Halal, the following conditions must be adhered to:

    a. The person who slaughters the meat must be a Muslim.

    b. The animal, while being slaughtered, should face Qiblah.

    c. The name of Allah (swt) must be uttered at the time of slaughtering.

    d. The throat of the animal must be cut with a

sharp instrument made of iron in a way that the jugular artery, jugular vein, esophagus canal and trachea are cut simultaneously.

4. Processed meat prepared in accordance with the dictates and teachings of the Qur'an are readily available through local commercial stores such as can be found in Bridgeport, Connecticut.

5. Islamic law requires that faithful Muslims abstain from eating or having any contact with pork, products derived from pork, foods seasoned with pork or its derivatives, and any other food items having come into contact with pork or pork bi-products.

6. Faithful Muslims can only use utensils which have never been used in the cooking, serving and consuming or pork or pork bi-products, or non-Halal meat products - unless the utensils have been purified as prescribed by Islamic law.

7. The Department of Corrections issues menus of the common fare food program which occasionally identifies those pork items included in the menu items but fails to identify food prepared from pork derivatives, such as certain gelatins and meat based fats.

8. Other religious groups are allowed to have their respective dietary requirements accommodated so they may observe their religious practices while maintaining a nutritionally - balanced diets that conforms to their respective religious laws and beliefs. For example, adherents of the Jewish faith are, on occasion, permitted to have specially prepared Kosher meat meals.

9. Plaintiffs have made repeated requests for similar

dietary allowances, or even the same, but have been consistently denied the same consideration and allowances accorded inmates of other faiths.

10. The defendants have denied the plaintiffs constitutional rights by failing to provide a nutritionally - balanced, prison provided diet which conforms to the requirements of Islamic law and meats acceptable health and medical guidelines.

11. The defendants failure to provide plaintiffs with Halal meat, to safeguard adequately against the pork contamination of other foods, to adequately and consistently identify pork and pork bi-products on the menus, forces the plaintiffs to eat a diet which lacks the daily nutrients and proteins required for proper nourishment.

12. Defendants failure to provide a "religiously adequate diet" severely curtails plaintiffs mealtime options. Plaintiffs complain that in adhering to their religious dietary restrictions they must eat repetitive meals of cereal, bread, peanut butter and vegetables.

REFERENCES

Academic American Encyclopedia. 1980. Arette Publication Co., Inc., Princeton, N.J.

Ali, Abdullah Yusuf. 1975. The Holy Qur'an, Text, Translation and commentary. The MSA of U.S. and Canada, Indianapolis, IN.

Bauer, W.W. 1965. Today's Health Guide, American Medical Association.

Benowicz, R.J. 1977. Non-Prescription Drugs and Their Side Effects, Grosset and Dunlap Co., N.Y.

Blakiston's Gould Medical Dictionary. 1979. A modern comprehensive dictionary in medicine, McGraw-Hill Book Co., N.Y.

Bricklin, M. 1976. The Practical Encyclopedia of Natural Healing, Rodale Press, Inc., Emmans, PA.

Burton, B.T. 1976. Human Nutrition, 3rd. ed., McGraw-Hill Co. N.Y.

Chaney, M.S. And M.L. Ross. 1971. Nutrition, 8th ed., The Houghton Mifflin Co., N.Y.

Christensin, H.E. et al. 1972. The Toxic Substances list, 1972 ed., U.S. Department of Health, Ed., Welfare.

Clark, R. L. And R.W. Cumley. 1973. The Book of Health, 3rd. ed., Van Nostrand Reinhold Co., N.Y.

De Holl, J.C. 1978. Encyclopedia of Labeling Meat and Poultry Products, 4th ed. Meat Plant Magazine Pub., St. Louis, MO.

Doty, W.L. 1973. Ed., All about Vegetables, Ortho Books, Chevron Chemical Company, San Francisco, CA.

Fomon, S.J. 1974. Infant Nutrition, 2nd ed., The W.B. Saunders Co., Philadelphia, PA.

Food Additives. 1971. Manufacturing Chemists Association, Inc., Washington, D.C.

Family Guide to Natural Medicine. 1993. The Reader's Digest Association, Inc., Pleasantville, New York / Montreal.

Guthrie, H.A. 1975. Introductory Nutrition, 3rd ed., The C.V. Mosby Co., St. Louis, MO.

Hall, R.L. 1973. Food Additives, Nutrition Today, 8 (4).

Handbook of Non-Prescription Drugs. 1979. 5th ed., Amer. Phar. Assoc., Washington, D.C.

Hulke, M., 1979. Editor, The Encyclopedia of alternative Medicine and Self-Help, Schocken Books, N.Y.

Kirschman, J.D. 1979. Nutrition Almanac, Nutrition Publ., Bismarck, ND.

Lagua, R.T. et al. 1974. Nutrition and Diet Therapy, Reference Dictionary, 2nd ed., The C.V. Mosby Co., St. Louis, MO.

Long, J.W. 1980. The essential Guide to Prescription Drugs, Harper and Row Pub., N.Y.

Marks, J. 1975. A Guide to the vitamins -- Their Role in Health and Disease, University Park Press, Baltimore, MD.

Merck Index. 1976. An Encyclopedia of Chemicals and Drugs, 9th ed., The Mercl and Co., Inc., Rahway, N.Y.

Miller, B.F. and C.B. Keane. 1987. Encyclopedia and Dictionary of Medicine, Nursing, and Allied Health, 4th ed., W.B. Saunders Company, Philadelphia, PA.

National Research Council, Food and Nutrition Board. 1974. Recommended Dietary Allowances, 8th ed., National Academy of Sciences, Washington, D.C.

Orten, J.M. and O.W. Neuhaus. 1975. Human Biochemistry, 9th ed., the C.V. Mosby Co., St. Louis, MO.

Pickthall, M.M. 1977. The Glorious Qur'an, Text and Explanatory Translation, Muslim World League, Pub., N.Y.

Qardawi. Y. 1972. Al-Halal Wal Haram Fil Islam (in Arabic), 6th ed., Al-Maktab Al-Islamic, Beirut, Lebanon.

Roody, P., et al 1977. Medical Abbreviations and Acronyms, McGraw-Hill Book Co., N.Y.

Roper, N. 1978. New American Pocket Medical Dictionary, Churchill, Livingston, N.Y

Sabiq, S. 1971. Fiqhus Sunnah, V.3 (in Arabic), Dar Al-Kitab Al-Arabi Beirut, Lebannon

Scarpa, L.S. and H.C., Keifer. 1978. Editor, Sourcebook on Food and Nutrition, 1st ed., Marquis Academic Media, Chicago,IL.

Shute, W.E. and H.J. Taub. 1971. Vitamin E or Ailing and Healthy Hearts, Pyramid House books, MD.

Stedman's Medical Dictionary. 1976. 23rd. Ed., The Williams and Wilkins Company, Baltimore, MD.

Stern, E.L. 1978. Prescription Drugs and Their Side Effects, Grosset and Dunlap Co., N.Y.

The Encyclopedia American. 1976. International Ed., 30 Volumes, American Corp. Pub., New York City, N.Y.

The New Encyclopedia Britannica (30 Volumes). 1979. Encyclopedia Britannica Inc., William Benton Publisher, Chicago, IL.

The Reader's Digest Association, Inc. 1982. Eat Better, Live Better, A Commonsense guide to nutrition and good health, Readers's Digest, Pleasantville, N.Y

Thomson, W.A.R. 1979. Black's Medical Dictionary, 32nd ed., Barnes and Noble Books, N.Y.

U.S. Medical Directory. 1977. 4th ed., U.S. Directory Service Pub., Miami, Fl.

Foundation for Islamic Knowledge

KNOWLEDGE

Islam emphaxized the important of knowledge to all mankind. It is only through true knowledge that one can appreciate the Creator of the Universe namely Allah (swt). Muslims are ordained to seek knowledge from cradle to grave and as far as a person can to obtain it.

In as much as seeking knowledge is a must on every Muslim, dessemination of knowledge is also incumbent on Muslims to the members of the society. The mehtods of disseminating the information should be lawful, as well as the truth is to be released to everyone. Hiding or keeping the true knowledge away from those who seek it, is considered a sin.

The best investment for every human being is through: perpetual charity (Sadaqa Jariya), useful knowledge that people shall benefit or, and a loving child who shall make special prayers for his/her parents.

LEGALITY

The Foundation has been established and registered with the

Secretary of the State of Illinoise since Janaury 8, 1987 as a non-profit, charitable, educational, religious and/or scientific society within th meaning of section 501 (c) (3) of the Internal Revenue Code.

The Foundation has a tax-exempt status with the IRS, and donations are considered tax-deductible.

FINANCES

The finances of the FOUNDATION are maily from donations and contributions in the form of cash, assets and wills.

INUMERENT OF INCOME

The purposes of the FOUNDATION are summarized as follows:

1. To promote Islamic Knowledge through education.
2. To create a better understanding of Islam among Muslims and non-Muslims throuygh education and communication.
3. To publish books and other literature about Islam and its teachings.
4. To desseminate Islamic Knowledge and education through, TV, Radio, Video, Audio and other means of mass communications.
5. To establish ecumenical among the religious people of America so that a better understanding will be created.

ACTIVITIES

The activities of the FOUNDATION shall include, but not be limited to the following:

1. Publishing literature pertaining to Islam.
2. Producing audio cassettes and audio-visual tapes on certain topics of Islam.
3. Giving lectures related to Islam as a religion, culture and civilization.
4. Cooperation with other societies, foundations and organizations whose aims and objectives are similar to the FOUNDATION.

KNOWLEDGE IN THE QUR'AN

The word knowledge ('ILM) is mentioned in the Qur'an more than 700 times in 87 different forms. Some of the pertinent Ayat are listed below.

1. The first Ayat revealed to Prophet Muhammad (pbuh) at Cave Hira' are in Surah Al-Alaq (The Clot) (96:1-5). They are related to knowledge of embroyology through scientific investigation.
2. Allah honors all those who knowledge. These people cannot be compared with the ignorant onees. See Surah Al-Zumar (The Troops) [35:28]
3. Only the knowledgeable people are those who do appreciate

Allah's (swt) creations. They are the ones who respect Him and worship Him with knowledge and humility. Please read Surah Fatir (The Creator) [35:28]

4. Knowledge is in the Hands of Allah and it is at His disposal. People are to seek the true knowledge from its source namely Allah. Read Surah Al-Mulk (The Sovereignty) [67:26].

5. People are to seek knowledge from Allah (swt) and are to ask Him to enrich them daily with 'ILM. Read Surah Taha [20:114].

KNOWLEDGE IN THE HADITH

Prophet Muhammad (pbuh) emphasized 'ILM tremendouly and encouraged Muslims to seek knowledge in any part of the world. The following is a summary:

1. In one Hadith the Prophet says: "The Knowledgeable people ('Ulama) are the inheritors to the Prophets."

2. In another Hadith He couraged Muslims to seek knowledge, saying: "Seeking knowledge is a must on every Muslim."

3. In another place, He demanded that knowledge is to be sought throughout lifetime, saying: "Seek knowledge from cradle to grave."

4. Knowledge is to be disseminated to all, and the best knowledge is that of the Qur'an, saying: "The best amongst you are the ones who learn Qur'an and teach it to others."

5. Knowledge is to be taught and to be carried on even after death. In His Hadith the Prophet said: "When a person dies, his deeds are over, except from three things; perpetual charity, a useful knowledge, or a good child who makes supplications for him."

The FOUNDATION will continue, with the help of Almighty God (Allah), to publish more useful literature. **With the generous help of the friends, The Foundation will be able to achieve its purposes, Inshaallah.**

FASTING
Regulations and Practices

Ahmad H. Sakr, Ph.D.

PUBLICATIONS by *AHMAD H. SAKR, Ph.D.*

BOOKS ABOUT FRIDAY KHUTAB:

* 1. Book of Al-Kutab
* 2. Islamic Orations
* 3. Orations from the Pulpit
* 4. Chronicle of Khutab
* 5. Friday Khutab
* 6. A Manual of Friday Khutab
* 7. Khutab Al-Masjid

BOOKS ON HEALTH, FOOD AND NUTRITION:

1. Dietary Regulations & Food Habits of Muslims
2. Overeating and Behavior
3. Islam on Alcohol
4. Alcohol in Beverages, Drugs, Food, & Vitamins
5. Cheese
6. AFTO and FAO
* 7. Fasting in Islam
8. Food and Overpopulation

	9.	Honey: A Food and a Medicine
	10.	Gelatin in Foods
	11.	Shortening in Foods
	12.	A Manual on Food Shortenings
*	13.	Pork: Possible Reasons for its Prohibition
	14.	Food Supplementation
	15.	World Health Organization for Muslim Nations
*	16.	A Muslim guide to Food Ingredients
	17.	Natural Therapeutics of Medicine in Islam (co-authored)
	18.	Islamic Dietary Laws & Practices (co-authored)
	19.	Food and Nutrition Manual (co-authored)
	20.	A Handbook of Muslim Foods
*	21.	Understanding Halal Foods: Myths and Realities

GENERAL SUBJECTS:

*	1.	Islamic Fundamentalism (co-authored)
*	2.	Du`a' After Completing the Recitation of Qur'an
*	3.	Introducing Islam to non-Muslim (co-authored)
	4.	Prostration - Sujood (new edition)
*	5.	Guidelines of Employment by Muslim Communities (co-authored)
*	6.	Farewell Khutbah of the Prophet - Its Universal

		Values
*	7.	Understanding Islam and Muslims
*	8.	Muslims and non-Muslims: Face to Face
*	9.	Matrimonial Education in Islam
*	10.	Life, Death and the Life After
*	11.	The Golden Book of Islamic Lists
*	12.	Al-Jinn
*	13.	Islam and Muslims: Myth or Reality
*	14.	Islamic Awareness
*	15.	Death and Dying
*	16.	Family Values in Islam

---

*   *These publications are available from:*
Foundation for Islamic Knowledge
P.O. Box 665
Lombard, IL 60148
Phone: (708) 495-4817 / Fax: (708) 627-8894

BOOKS TO BE PUBLISHED

1. The Adolescent Life
2. Islamic Perspectives
3. Islamic Understanding
4. Islam vs. Muslims
5. The Book of Healing
6. Speakers Bureau Guide Book
7. Islamic Shari`ah Text Book
8. Health, Hygiene and Nutrition
9. Halal - Haram Book of Khutab
10. The Book of Inquiries
11. Reflections from the Flying Falcon
12. Book of Du`a'
13. The Book of Targheeb
14. Scientific Reflections in the Qur'an
15. Biological Terms in the Qur'an
16. Family Counseling Guide Book
17. Educational Institutions in Islam
18. Writing an Islamic Will
19. Qur'an Commentary in Summary
20. Prostration (Sujood) - New Edition

These and other books will not be published unless someone like you comes forward and extend a hand of help. You may sponsor any of the above books; or any number of copies of a particular book.

Your help in any capacity is greatly needed even to pay the previous debts to the printers.

The Foundation is tax-exempted from the IRS and your donations are tax-deductible. The employer I.D. number with the I.R.S. is 36-352-8916.

For more information, or to send your donation, please contact:
Foundation for Islamic Knowledge
P.O. Box 665, Lombard, IL 60148, USA
Phone: (708) 495-4817 / Fax: (708) 627-8894

Books Available From the Foundation for Islamic Knowledge

Books Available From the Foundation for Islamic Knowledge

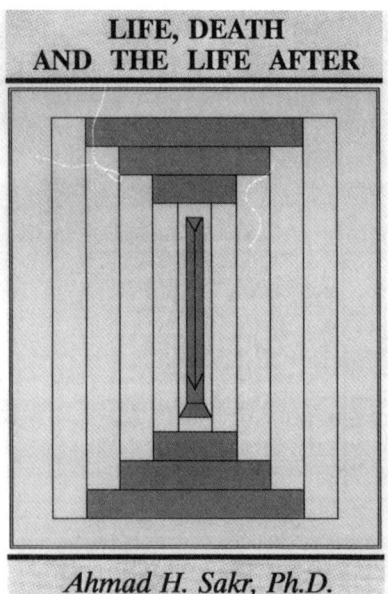

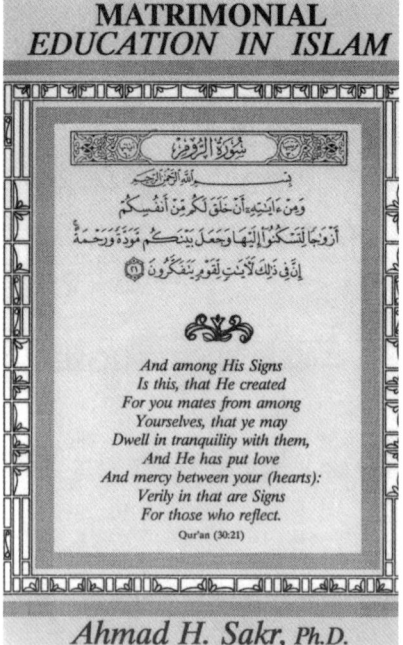

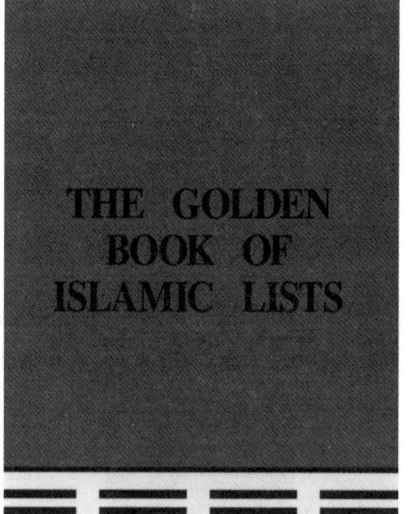

Books Available From the Foundation for Islamic Knowledge

Books Available From the Foundation for Islamic Knowledge

Farewell Khutbah of The Prophet ﷺ
Its Universal Values

KHUTAB AL-MASJID

AHMAD H. SAKR, Ph.D.

A Muslim Guide to Food Ingredients

AHMAD H. SAKR, Ph.D.
Professor of Nutritional Biochemistry